# T E N
# W H O
# L E F T

People Who Have Left
the Church and Why

## FRED CORNFORTH
### AND
## TIM LALE

**Pacific Press Publishing Association**
Boise, Idaho
Oshawa, Ontario, Canada

5165

Edited by Glen Robinson
Designed by Tim Larson
Cover art by Consuelo Udave
Typeset in New Century Schoolbook 11/13

Copyright © 1995 by
Pacific Press Publishing Association
Printed in the United States of America
All Rights Reserved

ISBN 0-8163-1298-2

95 96 97 98 99 • 5 4 3 2 1

# DEDICATION

This book is dedicated
to our friends and family
who share in the experience of the *Ten Who Left.*

# CONTENTS

# Foreword

The majority of those born into a Seventh-day Adventist family in North America in the post–World War II era have dropped out of the church. This has been especially true for white, Anglo Adventists—somewhat less so for African American Adventists of the Baby Boom generation—and appears to be a continuing trend in the generations following.

Others have measured the extent of this trend and indicated the major causes.* Fred Cornforth is the first to give personality and character to the stark statistics with a set of careful, honest case studies. As a young adult and youth consultant with seven years of pastoral experience, Cornforth takes a more relational view of the issue and introduces you to real people with names, faces, and feelings—the people behind the surveys and sociological studies others have published.

You will discover, as you read these personal stories,

that these "church dropouts" are your children and grandchildren or generational peers. They come from all kinds of families, and they are all kinds of people. Some have had their names dropped from the membership of the church; some are still members, even though they are inactive. Some have reestablished participation in the church, although in a different form than before.

These stories underline the very personal and unique nature of the faith experience of each individual. They defy easy categories and consistent theories. They provide evidence that the work of pastoral ministry, especially in the area of spiritual growth and faith development, requires a holistic view of the human being. For Adventists, this is, of course, the biblical view of humanity, yet it is often ignored in practice by Adventist pastors and leaders.

Many of the stories in this volume also demonstrate the key role of family life in faith development and congregational dynamics. For better or worse, childhood experiences and the example of parents determine much about a young adult's relationship with the church. Family ministries are often seen as "not evangelistic," but anyone reading Cornforth's case histories would have a hard time continuing to believe it. The dropout problem in the Seventh-day Adventist Church is, in fact, largely due to dualistic approaches to pastoral ministry and evangelism. When we learn to integrate faith with the nonreligious elements of personal life, we begin to build the kind of bond that will hold a much larger number of the youth reared in Adventist families.

More than anything, these are stories of grace! Some speak of the grace of the Lord Jesus Christ breaking through with the warmth of life when they confronted death and adversity on every side. Some tell of the infinite patience of the Holy Spirit, who stayed with them through rebellion and all the twists and turns of life to woo them back again. And some demonstrate the continuing mission of grace of the living God, who "would that not one be lost" among the people for whom He gave His life.

We speak of grace theologically far more often than we trace the contours of grace in the lives of individuals and families. And when we do take time to consider the work of grace in a life, it is often the heroic life of a rare individual. Here we are introduced to average, everyday people speaking of how they experience grace. In the telling of these stories, grace comes home to each of us in a striking way, and the presence of God in the most common aspects of life is affirmed.

These ten stories have many potential uses. Let me suggest a few that could enrich your life personally, as well as the small group or congregation you belong to.

1. The stories can be illustrations in sermons; preaching designed to educate for a more inclusive, hospitable, and accepting fellowship. In fact, each of these stories can be the centerpiece in a sermon, and an entire series of sermons might result, showing how a grace orientation can make a difference in each life.

2. The stories can be used as discussion starters for a small group or seminar series. Learning experiences for lay pastors, visitation teams, Sabbath School class leaders, or other local church officers can be enhanced by the use of these stories. Many times, wrestling with the reality of one person's real-life story is more instructive than theory presentations or skill-development exercises.

3. This book can be particularly useful for teams involved in reclaiming ministry. Many congregations have begun to work seriously to win back their inactive members as well as former Adventists living in the area. A key element is always a team of trained volunteers who make personal contacts and listen to the pain and frustration, as well as the hopes and dreams, of these individuals and through reflective conversation help them to sort out a new relationship with the church. These teams usually meet monthly to debrief their visits and pool their learnings. This book provides wonderful devotional material for such debriefing sessions!

4. As assigned, independent reading for elders and others involved in pastoral ministry, this book is an excellent tool to help prepare for the real thing. It suggests the range of situations and needs that each one of us involved in the practice of pastoring will encounter. It helps to focus methods and skills on the kinds of persons we minister to in Christ's name.

Beyond the practical uses for this volume, let me leave with you a plea that you read it prayerfully and with a compassionate, listening ear. These ten couples and individuals have something you must hear if you care about those for whom Christ died. They sketch the experience of two generations of Adventist youth, and unless we learn the lessons they have to teach, this tragedy will be repeated with even more generations.

The "second-generation" Adventist is a special kind of person. (By "second-generation," I mean all of us who grew up in an Adventist home, whether we be literally second, third, fourth, fifth, or even sixth in generations of Adventists in our family.) We often cannot point to a particular date for our conversion experience, and we do not have spectacular conversion stories to tell . . . just the fact that we learned about God each day of our lives. We have been well exposed to both the highest values and the worst cases of Adventist life and institutions. We know that Adventism is not perfect, but it is our home, our worldwide family, our mission and message. We are forever marked with "the blessed hope" of Christ's advent and that "temple in time," the Sabbath.

It is my prayer that the hundreds of thousands from my generation whose stories are so like the ten in this book will find again the joy and meaning that the Seventh-day Adventist Church can bring. Their stories of refound faith is another book waiting for Fred Cornforth to write. But it can't be written until you and I roll up our sleeves and make a difference in the lives of these people. Perhaps the whole story cannot be written until the new earth, but nonetheless, I want to see it written . . . I want to help make those stories happen!

Monte Sahlin
Assistant to the President
Seventh-day Adventist Church in North America

---

*For a complete bibliography of surveys and studies conducted in the last two decades by Seventh-day Adventist researchers, see "The Dropout Problem" by Monte Sahlin, a monograph available from the Office of Information and Research, headquarters of the Seventh-day Adventist Church in North America.

# Why Should We Care?

**H**igh-pitched drills screamed all around me as student dental hygienists practiced on one victim after another. I waited for Erin,[1] the student assigned to me, with my palms sweating. A friend of a friend had persuaded me to volunteer for some inexpensive dental care. Being a college student, I had succumbed to the allure of cheap treatment. I tried to console myself with the thought that an instructor was supervising the students.

Erin greeted me and began to explain the procedures she would follow. Her personable "drill-side" manner put me at ease. We made it through the checkup without any mishaps, and as I left, I felt that I could confidently face coming back to Erin for another visit.

My periodic visits for X-rays, cleanings, and gum inspections led to a friendship. After one visit, Erin began telling me about her background. She commented on the freedom she was experiencing at a public university compared with the limitations during her high-school education.

Then she dropped the bombshell.

"I'm a Seventh-day Adventist," she said. I was stunned. This university town had a small Adventist church, and I had been an elder there for two years. I had never noticed Erin at our services. As she continued, her story became clear. She had graduated from a Seventh-day Adventist academy in the West three years earlier and then left to make her own way. The church she still claimed as her own had not made any contact with her in the intervening years. Nor had she tried to contact her church.

I returned to Walla Walla College to finish my undergraduate degree about six months after that conversation, and I lost contact with Erin. Today, I have no idea where she is or what feelings she has for the Lord or her church.

The idea for writing this book began when I met Erin more than fourteen years ago. She has been in my thoughts often. In the years since she shared her story, several of my friends have stopped attending a Seventh-day Adventist church. I have accumulated some regrets for not having done more to help them face their challenges.

Chances are, you know people who have left the church too. A husband, wife, son, daughter, grandchild, friend. For some of us, the list is painfully long. It's happening often and everywhere—people severing their contact with the church or just drifting away. One study estimates that there may be one to two million former Seventh-day Adventists in North America alone.[2]

Erin's story represents hundreds of thousands of

people. But why have they left? What are their stories? Would they ever come back? *Ten Who Left* serves as a forum for Seventh-day Adventists to hear what's on the minds of those who have left.

## The Older Brother Syndrome

As you read the following stories, you may feel frustration or other strong emotions. Anger, confusion, helplessness, disappointment, and sadness are common emotional responses among active Adventists toward inactive or missing members. Please remember that these feelings are a natural response to one side of the story. This book allows ten former members to tell their side of the story and does not attempt to present a balanced survey of both the former members and those they left behind.

I believe most Adventists, upon honest reflection, can recall circumstances that might have led them to break contact with the church. But we are still here. All of us who remain active in the church should keep in mind the Older Brother Syndrome described in Luke 15.

Pride in having more spiritual moxie than those who have left represents one of the major barriers to reconciliation. When we nurture pride, it produces the most damaging emotion of all—resentment. One person's resentment may pool with the resentment of others in the same church, and the result is a wave of cool abandonment that washes away former or troubled members. No matter how strong the desire to repair these strained relationships on either side, resentment can cripple opportunities for reconciliation.

In our time, former brothers and sisters who try to return are often greeted only by a resentful "elder brother," which produces an exchange of verbal assaults. The former member decides to keep on traveling, never to return. Imagine the story of the prodigal son with a different ending. Instead of a brooding, resentful elder brother turning his back on the returning one, he joins his compassionate father as they run out together to meet the weary wanderer.

The only way to dodge the Older Brother Syndrome is to treat former members with the same unconditional concern we should show to every human being on the planet. We should allow them to explain themselves and then look for points at which we can begin reconciliation. Even though they may differ from some of our Adventist biblical and cultural expectations at a given moment, they will be encouraged to stay within the fellowship, continue to grow in Jesus' likeness as the Spirit moves them, and at the same time add richness to our faith community through a diversity of expression of our shared belief.

When you read these stories and you sense unaccepting feelings welling up inside you, stop and do an attitude check. You may be developing a case of the Older Brother Syndrome. If you give in to these feelings, you will end up judging each person by their absence instead of by the circumstances they encountered. Then your reading of the stories will yield only part of its reward.

When talking with a former or inactive Adventist, it is tempting to correct, add to, or edit their stories. What they need most, however, is an opportunity to vent without interruption or judgment. The fact that they still carry feelings deep inside them shows that they still care for the church. As you read their stories, try to listen. What we hear them say may move us to make personal and corporate changes that will create an environment where we all feel more welcome—and listened to.

## The Ten Who Left

We have known most of these individuals for years. Some we have known since we can remember. The five men and five women range in age from twenty-one to fifty-five. There are two couples, and the others are single or divorced. Some are married to non-Adventists. Some are converts, though most were raised as Adventists. They live in five different states stretching from the East to the West Coasts. They have been inactive for at least a year, and one person has been inactive for more than forty years.

Our relationships with these former members outside the interview environment have no doubt influenced our telling of their stories. Some might consider this a weakness, but friendship allowed us to set a tone of trust and acceptance as they opened up painful, vulnerable parts of their lives. Each person interviewed has approved the final version of their story.

Why not interview ten people who left the church and then returned? That's a good question and deserves a good answer. This book is about what goes on inside the mind of a former member who has not found a solution to their problem with the church. It is necessary to hear from those who have not come back into the fellowship. A good sequel to *Ten Who Left* may be *Ten Who Returned*.

---

1. Not her real name. All names in this book have been changed to protect the privacy of former members.
2. Monte Sahlin, *The Dropout Problem in the Adventist Church in North America*. North American Division Church Ministries Report (Silver Spring, Md.: North American Division of Seventh-day Adventists, 1989).

---
Chapter 1 ───────

# LindsEy

**Age: Thirty-something**
**Occupation: Corporate vendor**
**When she left the church: 1978**


**Are you a Christian?**
Yes.

**What denomination do you consider yourself affiliated with?**
Seventh-day Adventists. It's all I have ever known or been.

**Would you consider yourself a good Adventist?**
No.

**Why?**
Because I smoke. I don't go to church. I am not active or involved.

**How long have you been inactive? Do you remember when you stopped attending?**
Somewhere right after I left academy. I went to an SDA college for a little while. I couldn't do it. I didn't want to be there. I just went there because all of my friends went there. That's where you went to find your

husband and live happily ever after.

**You did eventually marry. Where did you meet your husband?**

In a bar.

**Did you feel guilty because you were marrying a non-Adventist?**

At that point, it didn't enter my mind. I had been inactive for quite a while. It didn't really matter that much to me.

**Do you remember the events that led up to your becoming inactive?**

In college, my roommate and I would go places on the weekends. We would go to the beach, the mountains, and home. We would leave early Saturday morning and miss church. We didn't really party. We just never made it to church. I was about nineteen or twenty when this all happened. I enjoyed going to church—what I remember of it.

Even now I wake up on Saturday morning, and I think, *I should go to church*, because that's the way I was raised for eighteen or nineteen years. I guess I miss the social part the most—going where other people are. When I moved out of the house and got my own place, I started making new friends. They weren't Adventists.

As I drifted away, I got involved in social things that occupied my time. I started drinking in academy, but not a lot. I started smoking when I was twenty-two or twenty-three, but I had already stopped attending church. I also started drinking more and did some pot. By twenty-four or twenty-five, I was doing the hard stuff.

**Did anyone other than family members ever visit you after you left the church?**

No.

**Are your parents divorced?**
Yes, when I was twelve or thirteen, they divorced. I felt devastated for a while. But I always felt I was loved. Especially by my dad. It seemed like he was always there. When I got off drugs and went to a counselor, she made me realize that I had a lot of issues to work out with my mom.

**Today, one of your parents is an active Adventist, and the other isn't, right?**
Yes. My mom was an Adventist because that's what she was supposed to be. It's like me when I went to college, because that's where everybody went to get married. That's where she met Dad. He was planning to work for the church. I know that she is a Christian, and she believes in God. With my dad, it's more obvious. He tells me all the time that he is praying for me. They both believe in God. They just show it in different ways.

**How were you as a teenager? Were you able to make your own decisions growing up?**
Yes and no. My parents were pretty cool about allowing me to make my own decisions. I went to Adventist schools all the way through up to college. Because of the controlled environment, I didn't have to make a lot of decisions—they were already made for me. In some ways, I think about the way I was treated as being a type of brainwashing. You were told what was OK and what wasn't. I did not like that part.

When I did get freedom, I went wild. Nuts. My life was fun but insane. Even dangerous. Guns getting pulled, getting arrested, fights—all that stuff made my life more intense and crazy.

Now, I realize that I have an addictive personality. I am an alcoholic. Sometimes I still feel drawn toward drugs. When I used them, drugs were more important than family, food, or sex.

I still smoke. I want to quit; I'm just not ready. I'm still working on the issues of drugs and alcohol. I think about quitting all the time. I'm almost ready.

**Picture yourself coming back to your home church this next Sabbath. What would be going through your mind?**

The older members, I feel, would judge me. Though most of them wouldn't, I still think some of them would. I could relate, however, to younger people if they were around. They seem to be more accepting.

The services are too structured. I don't feel like I could relax. I would be trying to remember what we are supposed to do next: Are we supposed to stand, sit, kneel, pray, sing, or what?

Also, they still sing the same songs we sang when I was a kid. It's so structured. I couldn't feel relaxed. A church that is more relaxed and accepting would be very attractive.

**Have you thought about going back to church?**

I have thought about it a lot. I have attended church services several different places. I liked it very much. I know I should be attending church; it's just not that important to me.

**Why is it important to attend church?**

Not to please anyone, that's for sure. I guess because it's good for you—the fellowship, the support to keep going. I'm not saying that everyone who goes to church is a good Christian either. Some people go to church to show off their clothes or to see the plaque that shows how much they gave for the new organ. That's not church. It's almost a fashion show.

**If Jesus were to come right now, what would He think when He sees you?**
A mixed-up kid. Not a bad person.
**What are you going to do when you see Him?**
I am probably going to faint! [*Laughter*] I know in the back of my mind that He is coming. I just keep putting it off. I know that I am not ready to go to heaven.
**What do you have to do to go to heaven?**
Stop smoking, for one thing. It's not good for me, and I think it is really important that I take care of myself. I also think that I need to go to church—for me, because that's what you are supposed to do. I also need to pray more so I can grow closer to Him.
I pray now. When I'm driving in town and I go by someone's house and I know they have drugs, I have to pray to keep myself from going in. Not so much for the people, but because of the drugs. I don't do "alone" very well. I miss those people. They were my friends. I am driving down the road, and I want to see them. I miss their companionship. If I stop to see them, though, I know that drugs will be there. I pray and keep on driving, but I miss my friends.
**What do you think of when you hear the word *salvation*?**
Being saved.
**How do you get "saved"?**
I don't know.
**Were you prepared, within the environment that you were raised in, to live in the real world?**
Not at all. Not at all. The world is good and bad. The world I was raised in was a school environment—it was a good life, but it was unrealistic. I did not know how to act out in the real world. It was fun, but I definitely

found the good and the bad.

**Do you want your children to be Seventh-day Adventist?**

I have never thought about it. I want them to be exposed to it. I don't know that I want them involved in it. It's not bad to be an Adventist—I just want them to have a choice. They have been exposed to just about everything in the world, the good and the bad. I just want them to have a choice.

**What do you think of Ellen G. White?**

I think she was a prophetess. She had some really good things to say. But that was then. A lot of people misuse her. I don't think she would have liked that.

**If you could, what would you change in the church?**

Older people who run the church are really hung up on a bunch of stuff. They say "E. G. White says . . ." The world has changed a whole lot since she was alive. But they haven't changed. They have become irrelevant. The church does not relate to the 1990s. A lot of E. G. White's writings could be updated and still be true to her principles. It could be done. It needs to be done.

Doctrinally speaking, I still believe in the Sabbath and that when you die you are asleep. I don't think God judges us on whether we eat meat or not.

**Do you see yourself coming back someday?**

Yes. I see myself trying to become an active member. I don't know really what that means, but the church would have to be very accepting and patient with me. The people mean a lot to me.

## THOUGHT QUESTIONS

1. Lindsey mentions that the social aspects of church are what she misses most. Yet no one visited her when she left the church. How can we explain this apparent contradiction?

2. What is your reaction to Lindsey's comment about how decisions were made for her? What can we do for young adults that provides an environment where they learn to make decisions on their own?

3. What can the church do to help those who struggle with substance abuse? Some have suggested that the church has denied there is a problem with alcoholism and drug addiction. Do you agree or disagree?

4. Is Lindsey justified in being concerned about members judging her if she were to come back to church? What about her comments about the way we worship? Are her observations valid?

5. Lindsey has a view of salvation that is based on her own behavior. Is she understanding salvation correctly? Where did she learn this view of salvation?

# Chapter 2

# JAMES

**Age: Thirty-something**
**Occupation: Health-care administrator**
**When he left the church: 1987**

**How would you describe your upbringing?**

It was very strict. Everything was based on one principle, it seems like—"my parents' way or the highway."

**How would you characterize a "strict" upbringing?**

You have to understand; my father was an attorney, and my mother was a schoolteacher. It had a lot to do with her strictness—his, too—but mostly hers. She allowed us to interact with the neighbors, but it was very controlled. We were prevented from attending birthday and swimming parties. They had very little tolerance for non-Adventists. Saturday night, we would sit waiting for the sun to go down to light the fire in the fireplace, because it wouldn't be right to start it before sundown.

Once when I was at college, my dad told me not to call on Sabbaths because we might end up talking about things we shouldn't talk about during those "sacred hours." That hurt me. It told me that Sabbath was more important to my dad than I was.

I guess you could sum it up by saying that if it doesn't fit into their picture of what is right, you're wrong. No questions asked. They treated their non-Adventist acquaintances the same way. If they didn't agree with them, they backed away. It really amazed me that they could feel that way, because it cut them off from the very people they could have helped. In religion, it isn't right or wrong; it's whom you can help.

**How would you describe your relationship with your parents?**

Somewhat strained. My mother keeps fueling the tension. She always says, "I know you'll do what's right someday, by coming back to church," as if not going to church was wrong. Both my mom and my dad were zealots. Giving offerings was more important than food. Church duties always came first and family second.

I have watched my mom, motivated by low self-esteem, work so hard for the church that she would get sick. She tried to make up for it. It's almost as if she believed that if she did anything for herself, she was being selfish. So she never took the time to work through her problems. Instead, she tried to cover them up. I really feel sorry for her. She was raised in a dysfunctional family. Rather than deal with problems, she swept them under the rug. She dealt with us that way too.

**Tell me about the events that led up to your leaving the church.**

It started at college. I spent a lot of money and got an average education. The variety and content were average. Professors were very dedicated, but their experience was mostly within the world of Adventism. Few of them had any experience in the real world. In fact, their view of the world was unrealistic. They didn't prepare me for the real world at all.

Then my marriage ended in divorce. It was a really difficult period for me. I went to them [the church] for help and didn't find any real resources to assist struggling marriages. My single biggest issue with the church was my cry for help—that no one answered. No one visited. No one called. Only two people invited me over to their home for dinner. I tried twice, and then I gave up.

At church, no one asked what we needed. They just wanted to know if it was her fault or my fault. The average member was almost ignorant on how to handle cries for help. We had two or three friends going through the same problems.

Then rumors surfaced about me, saying that I had had affairs. Specific names of women were even circulated, but I didn't do any of it. My wife knew that none of it was true, but because the pastor did nothing to stop the rumors, many people didn't believe me.

The straw that broke the camel's back was when they took away my church duties. "You have too many problems to help us out" was the message I got. This happened to other members too—some of them close friends of mine.

At this point, I started playing games with the church. I'd miss one Sabbath just to see if anyone noticed. At first, they did, but I didn't feel any comfort or nurture during this time. Then I'd miss two Sabbaths. No one seemed to notice. There came a time when I started getting more help from non-Adventist Christians than Adventists. They seemed much more capable of helping me through this tough time. I needed them, and they were there.

**What changes would you like to see in the church? What in the church would draw you back?**

Very little attention is focused on how to live from day to day. We need less emphasis on doctrine and more time on relationships. How do you get along in life? How do you work out conflict at work? In your personal life? What does the Bible say about those things?

I would encourage self-improvement courses that were biblical. We were raised to think that it's not good to build yourself up. You must be humble and meek. Thus, you end up walking through life with low self-esteem but patting yourself on the back because you are spiritual. That doesn't make sense to me.

Also, I would encourage more social activities away from church—to get to know [members] in a more informal way. The social is as important as the God relationship because He gave us each other.

This brings me to two important issues: the role of women and our attitude toward homosexuals. I was raised to believe, as was my sister, that women need to be submissive. Even in the wedding vows, women are told to submit. Women seem to have a more caring or nurturing side than most men. There is a huge need in the church for female ministers. It's almost as if our church environment has said to us that this is not so. It took me a while in my work relationships to value women for their uniqueness and strength. It was as if they were one level below men. I am still working on this. It doesn't matter what some people might think. Women are equals—more than equals—because of what they bring to humanity.

With regard to homosexuals—my wife [James has remarried] and I know several gays and lesbians. But I wouldn't feel comfortable bringing our friends to an SDA church. I know my parents would not tolerate it. It's so black and white to them and many church members. It's either right or wrong, and unless you see it their way, you're wrong. Who cares who is right and wrong when those who claim to be right are judgmental? I couldn't care less about 1844! On the other hand, how do I cope? How do I help my homosexual friends?

Everything comes down to an "us versus them," "right versus wrong." How come the church can't take the lead and call it an us-us or win-win situation? I learned that from the business world, not the church.

The last area I would change would be the attitude toward Catholics. We have been taught that they are bad. I was raised thinking that they were evil. It was an evil empire. I attended a Jesuit college for my MBA, and I really enjoyed being around them. I feel that I can really relate to them. Their commitment to the Christian way of life was as strong as any Adventist's. My parents were mostly responsible for this incorrect view, but the church seems to nurture this attitude also. Some of my closest friends are Catholic. We just need to realize that people from different backgrounds can both be right. It's not right versus wrong or good versus evil; it's about our relationships with each other and with God.

**What changes need to take place in your life?**
I am still deprogramming myself on several attitudes.

Especially with this concept about not being right all the time. I guess I need to accept that people in the church are just as human as I am. They may say things that are ignorant, but not out of a lack of love. They are people just like me.

I would also have to do a better job of balancing my opinions with the church's beliefs. I am not willing to do this, especially with the way we treat gays and lesbians. I wasn't raised to be a leader; I was raised to be a follower. I would have to be a leader. I caved in on areas I held convictions on. I would need to be strong enough to hold my own beliefs while holding on to the important things of Adventism. It would take a different kind of commitment than I have ever had.

**How would it differ?**

Commitment from the heart rather than what I thought my family and friends believed. At this point in my life, I have to be personally committed to get involved in something, including church.

**Do you see anything in the church worth committing yourself too?**

Probably not.

**What was the last contact you had from the church?**

The last contact I had was from an Adventist college. They asked me for money. It took me almost ten years to pay off my mediocre education [student loans], and they still want me to give them money.

**Any closing thoughts?**

I feel a lot of sorrow not being in the church. I also feel disillusioned. Since I left the church, however, I feel that I have learned to get along with people better. I have a better self-image and a more positive outlook on life. I am much more open-minded.

Also, I was recently elected president of a local Kiwanis club. I feel that I am really involved in a better way. Passing out literature is one thing, but helping hungry kids is something altogether different. Is it more important to quote texts, roll out the scroll, or answer positively the question, "Did you help someone today?" Are people better off because you are part of their lives? After all, what really matters in life? The essence of Christianity to me is about building relationships with others.

## THOUGHT QUESTIONS

1. James's family was very strict. Why do you think his parents raised him that way? What effect did this have on his life?

2. Do you think James and his sister's upbringing is unique in Adventist circles?

3. Why didn't the church hear James's cries for help? Was he wrong to play games with the church? How do you feel about the church asking him to resign his church offices?

4. How do you feel about the areas of change for the church James points out? Do you agree? What would you add? Is there an acceptable compromise?

5. What do you think about James's comments about deprogramming himself? What does he mean?

6. Why would someone develop a better self-image outside the church? Or get along with people better outside the church?

---- Chapter 3 ----

# Jackie

**Age: Twenty-something
Occupation: Police dispatcher
When she left the church: 1991**

**Tell me about your background.**

My parents converted to Adventism when I was a year old. My mother was baptized, but my father struggled with smoking. He was able to quit smoking for about six weeks but was denied baptism. Church members said they wanted to make sure he was really over his habit. To this day, he will defend Seventh-day Adventism, though he has never totally sensed the church community's acceptance. In a sense, we were raised in an Adventist home.

I have one sister and two brothers. We each attended several years of church school. One brother still goes to church, plus my mom.

**Do you consider yourself an Adventist still?**

Yes, but not very active.

**What was it like to be an active Adventist?**

Things really started changing when I began smoking. I had a ton of stressors in my life. On Friday afternoons, I would race home from shopping to vacuum and cook food for Sabbath. Then I did several things to get ready for church. I would smoke one last cigarette on Friday night. I would take a shower that night and another Sabbath morning to get all the smell of smoke off me. I would wash my clothes and use scented dryer sheets to remove any trace of smoke from them. I would go through my house and open up all the windows to freshen up my place. Before going off to church, I would put on perfume. No one seemed to notice at church, though one of the elders may have known. He was also my dentist.

After church, my limbs would start to shake. I would race home to get a cigarette. It tasted so good. I remember thinking to myself, *I can't keep this up for long*. But then I would relax because I wouldn't have to worry again until next Friday.

**Did smoking cause you to leave the church?**

It was part of it. I had a whole bunch of things come down on me all at once. In a one-month period, I got overwhelmed. It was Christmastime, and I learned that my parents were getting a divorce. I filed for bankruptcy that season, and I was diagnosed as manic-depressive. I lost my main job (I had two jobs trying to pay off my debts) in a disagreement over my work schedule. My boss wanted me to work Sabbaths. He told me that unless I worked Saturdays, my work environment would become difficult. When he learned that I had been diagnosed as manic-depressive, he used that against me. He said it made me unfit for work. Also, my room-mate was behind on her part of the rent, and we got evicted.

During this time, I slowly began slipping away. Over several weeks, I began to withdraw. I was working at the time in the cradle roll department, editing the church newsletter, hosting a women's meeting in my home, and singing special music at least once a month. I was really involved.

You might say the scales were tipped when the community services center director insisted that I help her by getting more involved. I tried several times to tell her that I was too busy. When I told her No, she fired back, "Some Christians have time to help out their church." I couldn't believe it. Didn't she know what I was already doing? Didn't she know how much stress I was under? I thought to myself, *If she hasn't noticed what I've been doing, I wonder if I am really needed.* I already had tons of stress. I sure didn't need another thing.

What is so odd with all this stuff is that I remember having an intense spiritual experience three months before. I was walking along the surf when I felt this strong emotional response to God. I remember promising Him that I would never turn my back on Him—ever.

**What happened next?**

This might sound odd, but smoking became the only thing I looked forward to. It relaxed me. It also helped curb my appetite, and I started to lose weight. You might say that I began to justify smoking based on the benefits it gave me.

For days, I would do nothing but eat and sleep. I was completely exhausted from stress that I could do nothing about. You might say that I not only stopped attending church; I stopped living. I was motivated out of self-preservation to remove all the negative forces in my life—including church.

**Do you think you will ever come back to church?**

I can't count the number of times I have laid out my clothes the night before. I just never follow through. I think to myself, *They are finishing Sabbath School now,* or *I wonder who is at the fellowship dinner today.* After church is over, I feel bad. I should have gone.

I would probably have come back already if I didn't smoke. I realize that comment sounds like an excuse. Smoking to me is something really dirty. Getting caught smoking would be like getting caught reading a dirty magazine. There is something perverse about smoking.

If I did return, I would live under the constant fear that I would be discovered and then rejected. I worry that if they learn I am smoking, they will remove my name from church membership. I saw one guy removed from the books. They treated him roughly. I don't want that to happen to me.

**Why is your membership so important to you?**

I equate church membership with salvation. I know that's not right. However, I think it anyway. I don't want to lose my membership. I am a Seventh-day Adventist. If someone removed my membership, I would be devastated.

**Has anyone been to visit you since you left?**

No.

**When was your last Adventist contact?**

I was working at a police station one Saturday, when a young man came in to report an accident. As he described the accident to me, he lit up a cigarette. During the interview, he mentioned that since it was a church trip, there was a special insurance policy. When he showed me the proof-of-insurance form, I was blown away to see that the policy was for the Seventh-day

Adventist church. I told him that I was an Adventist too. Almost at the same time, we caught each other staring at the other's cigarette. He told me his pastor was aware of his problem and was working with him on it.

**What changes would you like to see in the church?**

Something that bothers me is people talking about adornment all the time. I wear my ninety-nine-cent earrings, and they wear suits or dresses I could never afford. The church places these individuals in leadership positions, while people with inexpensive earrings are discussed at church boards. Something is wrong.

Also, dancing is mentioned in the Bible in lots of places. While I believe there are wrong forms of dancing, some dancing is biblical. I think such rigid beliefs on dancing and jewelry are garbage.

Most importantly, I have always heard that the church is like a hospital for sick people, but I have never seen a church like that. The church needs a more tolerant view of people and their problems. Right now, church is a place you go after you have your act together. I just don't feel comfortable in that kind of environment of perfection I sense at church. Don't get me wrong; I need to change too. I need to stop smoking, and then I will feel comfortable enough to come back. Sometimes I think I'm strong enough to quit. Other times I think God must look down at me and think that I'm the world's biggest weakling.

## THOUGHT QUESTIONS

1. Do you think a lot of people live a secret life like Jackie? Why?

2. What kind of response, if any, should Jackie have given the community services director?

3. How can we help people like Jackie not see church as another stressor in their lives?

4. Why do people who smoke feel as if they can't come back to church?

5. How do you feel about Jackie's beliefs on jewelry and dancing?

6. Should a church be like a hospital for the sick? If so, how can we treat the sick without condemning them?

---

Chapter 4 —————

## GEORGE

**Age: Fifty-something**
**Occupation: Small-business owner**
**When he left the church: 1950s**

**Even though you left the church at the age of
fifteen, you have tried to come back several times.
Your first attempt happened shortly after you
were married. Tell us about that experience.**

I married a non-Adventist, and she was interested in
going to church. We arrived on Sabbath morning, and
several individuals there knew my family name because
some of my relatives are well known in the denominational work. The Sabbath School superintendent approached my non-Adventist wife and asked her to give
the mission story the next week. She thanked the person
for the opportunity but declined. She didn't even know
what the mission story was.

When we returned the next week, the person would
not take No for an answer. My wife was left standing in
the parking area after church, holding the story that she
was supposed to present the next Sabbath. So, the next

week we didn't show up, and no one read the story.

**Have you tried to come back since then?**

Not with my wife. I have tried on several other occasions. It is always the little things that stop you from going back. It's an excuse, more than anything. When my name was taken off the books, I had been a member of an academy church. After I left the area, I got a letter from them saying that if I didn't transfer my membership in a given amount of days, because of requirements of one thing or another, my name would be dropped from the rolls. Time went by, and I didn't transfer, so I wasn't part of the church anymore.

The reason I'm not an Adventist today is this. As you're growing up in an Adventist home, you're taught to pray a certain way; you're taught that things are done a certain way. You're taught that you go to church and follow the Bible, but you are not taught how these things can become part of your everyday life. Going away to academy at thirteen, all of a sudden you don't have leadership from home at all. I discovered that I could eat a hamburger and not die. I went to a movie and didn't go to hell. Life went on. I learned that I went to work, not to set an example of being a good Christian, but to earn a living.

Everything I had done early in life was to be a Christian. My career direction was to be a denominational employee. That was the scope of my life—it was a very narrow one. That was my parents' prerogative. But it didn't answer the questions I ran into. So I had to fill in the blanks on my own. It made it tough on my wife and kids because I went through quite a learning process over time.

You take a step toward the things you've been taught were wrong and realize that they aren't fatal. Consequently, the value of them as a negative, as a deterrent, isn't as strong. So you reevaluate the criteria that direct your life.

That was it in a nutshell. No one's neglect. No neglect at all. It's just the way circumstances were and the way I dealt with them.

**When you left the church, did anyone visit you or attempt to contact you?**

No, not with our family name they wouldn't.

**Have you had any contacts with Adventism outside your family?**

Two people over the years have contacted us about returning. A pastor came out one time and said, "I just want you to know that fly fishermen can go to heaven too." That statement really made an impact on me. It was a different view of God than I had been brought up with. Forty years ago, you wouldn't be allowed in heaven because you were wasting your time on earthly things.

A while back a second person contacted me who had been baptized by one of my relatives. He called and wanted to know how I was doing. I had known him for several decades. He said that he would like to be invited to the next family get-together. I said I would be glad to invite him. He then asked me for my address, because he wanted to stop and say Hi sometime. So I told him.

Less than one week went by, and the mail started coming. All kinds of announcements. The old "gotcha" bit. "You have to come to this," or "You have to come to that," "Your uncle means a lot to me, and this means a lot to him," and this kind of stuff.

**How did you react to this kind of mail?**

This stuff I've seen before. The Revelation Seminar was one of them. We just file-thirteened it. As a result, we didn't bother to call this guy back when we had a family get-together. He contacted us using family as bait, but there was a hook. I call that false pretenses. But I grew up in an environment where this type of activity was common.

I remember sitting with a church member somewhere waiting for people he wanted to study with to stick their head out the window so he could nail them with a Bible study they didn't want. To him, it was important that they not get away. To me, it became another reason I didn't want anything to do with the church.

**What would you change in the church if you could?**

We moved one time, and I wanted to get back into church but not the traditional way. I wanted to get to know the people slowly, in a neutral environment. I enjoyed volleyball a lot, but when I called around asking if any church in the area had a volleyball night, I couldn't find one. I was even laughed at by some—especially the older generation.

I just wish more churches had programs like the Mormons do. Not as a recruitment tool, but as a family activity that is fun. That helps to give a more balanced picture of God than just sitting in church in a tweed-wool suit and listening to long, boring sessions.

When I was a kid living near an Adventist college, they offered all kinds of activities such as concerts, symphonies, and other things. My mother wanted to go, but my dad considered it a waste of time. Church and life should be fun sometimes.

**Is there anything else you would change?**

In all fairness, not a lot. In my case, it was bad timing.

**In what way was it bad timing? What happened**

**to you when you left?**
At academy, I always had to get up early in the morning because I worked at the bakery. I would get up at 4:00 a.m. and work until 7:00. By the time we got out of our work clothes and got out of the bakery, it was 7:15 a.m. Worship was at 7:00 a.m. and lasted until 7:20. I was working my way through school and trying to be independent. I didn't want my folks, who were denominational employees, to have to put money up for my schooling. In the afternoon and early evening, I worked a second job in the laundry. Between the two jobs, I was working six to eight hours a day.

A member of the faculty had told me I did not need to attend morning worship because there was no way I could make it. One day I got a call from the dean because I had missed several worships. Actually, I hadn't been to one in six weeks.

I explained to the dean what I had been doing. He said that it didn't matter. To him, it was a point of discipline. To me, it was unfair. How was I supposed to be at work doing my job and still be at worship? For punishment, he assigned me free labor. I had to prep desks for painting by sanding them. One for each worship I had missed. It took about three hours to sand each desk by hand. By doing free labor, I was going to lose the equivalent of one month's wages. My family couldn't afford it.

Throughout the next week, I continued to work at the bakery and the laundry as usual. I was trying to sort things out. I went to a faculty member and tried to appeal the dean's decision, but they just referred me back to the dean.

I can't remember if it was Sunday or Monday, but I was working in the laundry at 7:00 or 8:00 at night. The

dean came in and confronted me about not being in
study hall. I explained to him that my parents were
denominational employees and didn't have much and
that I needed to build up some extra hours so I could do
the free labor.

He made a grab at me to shake me. When he did, I
came over his arms and hit him. He was shocked. Most
kids knuckled under to his authority, but I didn't know
him well enough for him to break me. I popped him right
in the forehead, of all places. I was just swinging.

I left. I didn't run. I walked to my room and packed my
suitcase. I set it right by the door. The next morning, I
was on the first bus out of there. I paid my own way.
That's the reason why I left academy at fifteen. That was
the last time I had anything significant to do with the
Seventh-day Adventist Church.

**What changes do you feel need to take place in
you before coming back to church?**

It's like quitting smoking—you have to want to. After
so many years, I guess I don't want or need to be close to
anyone other than the family and friends we have now.

On the other hand, it would be nice to be doing
something for others. The next question is who? And
what?

**What do you think of heaven and eternal life?**

Heaven is not a big goal for me. We don't work toward
it. Helping others is important to us. We have been
involved in various financial ways with the Salvation
Army. That's spiritual to me.

Eternal life is attractive to me, but I don't equate
heaven with eternal life. I would like to be with God.
However, He is different than I was raised to believe. He
is not an ogre. Eternal life is like Thanksgiving or

Christmas. It's family time. My family is my life—my religion. My dad's life was his religion. That's the main difference between us.

**What is your relationship with God?**

I believe everything the SDA Church teaches. The system is where I have problems. I just don't follow them in my life. When I hear the old hymns, I still well up inside. It bridges the gap between then and now.

**Do you feel guilty about your life and your inactivity?**

No, not anymore.

**Do you consider yourself a Seventh-day Adventist?**

No. I just have not found a religion that compels me to become more involved.

5165

# THOUGHT QUESTIONS

1. It's easy to assume that family members of well-known Adventists are active. How should we respond to such individuals who are not? What does this incident tell us about inviting people to be involved in church activities before we get to know them?

2. How do you feel about the way George's membership was dropped?

3. Is it possible to protect young people from the world so much that they develop an unrealistic view of God and life?

4. What do you think of the motives of the two who contacted George? Did the pastor show good judgment by making the comment about fly-fishing? How can George's reaction to the mail he received help us judge the effect of reclamation projects?

5. Experts in reclaiming ministry tell us that inactive members can recall the details of discouraging encounters as if they happened yesterday. How could the academy staff have responded differently to George's situation? How could George have handled the situation better?

# Chapter 5

# Rick and Kari

**Age: Forty-something**
**Occupation: Attorney, homemaker**
**When they left the church: 1986**

**Kari, tell me about your family background.**
My parents divorced when I was very young. My father was very abusive, and my mother had to get out. She was afraid something might happen to her children. My dad paid child support of forty dollars a month to help raise four children ages six to ten. He stopped paying after the first year. As a result, my mother worked two and three jobs to keep food on the table and us in church school. I feel, sometimes, as though I lost both my father and mother then.

In an attempt to be mother and father to us, my mother ran a very strict home. She stressed perfection in every aspect of life. Ellen White was quoted often. TV and radio were not allowed in our home.

But you know, in spite of her strictness, I have a great deal of admiration for her stamina and commitment, for wanting to raise her children right. She loved us and wanted the best for us.

I traveled to an Adventist academy at fourteen. I really enjoyed it there because I had lots of friends. I wanted to be there rather than home because, in some ways, I had more freedom. I missed not having my horse because he was still at home. He had been my way of getting away from it all.

Though my experience at school was good generally, there were some drawbacks. Academy life did nothing to prepare me for real life. In fact, the more I was there, the more I grew afraid of the outside world, because we were told constantly that they [the faculty] were protecting us from the world.

One rule that I will never forget was that all girls had to wear bras—whether they needed them or not. The principal would go around sticking his hands up girls' shirts to see if they had one on!

At school, I dated here and there, and at sixteen I began dating this one guy. We got very serious. In time, we became sexually intimate. When that happened, my life was changed forever. My environment taught me that now that I've slept with this guy, I'm going to stick with him. At eighteen, two years later, I married him—mostly out of the religious commitment I felt I needed to uphold. Little did I realize the impact my future divorce would have on the very religious convictions I sought to uphold by marrying him.

**Rick, tell us about your background.**

My parents were much older than most when they had me. They ran their home very strictly. They were very judgmental. To keep peace in the family, I went along with the game, though it really made me angry.

In other ways, I feel like I had a real advantage over

others because I was raised in a type of Mecca of Adventist education. I went to our schools from first grade all the way through to graduate school. I believe I received a superior education—though I do agree with Kari's observations. I was so protected from the outside world that when I got out of school, I didn't know how to relate.

I have one sister, who is the oldest child, and an older and younger brother. I get along well with my sister and her husband. They, too, are former Adventists. Even though they don't go to church, they have real Christian hearts.

My relationship with my two brothers is much, much different. My younger brother, who is an unemployed professional, has kept looking to me for financial help. I have tried, but nothing seems to help him. It became so disappointing that I ended up having to pull away from him. He has grown increasingly self-centered and doesn't realize that true happiness and self-esteem come from helping others. I can't reach him. God doesn't help those who can help themselves. He helps the helpless.

My older brother was my idol while I was growing up. He was a real super jock in college. I really looked up to him. When I went through my divorce, it redefined our relationship. He knew why I was going through divorce, but he didn't have the fortitude to accept it because of his religious fervor. He couldn't deal with the fact that my marriage was finished, and that hampered him because he couldn't separate his emotions from his religion. He couldn't deal with what I was going through.

He is a good but very rigid guy. He unfortunately allowed his religious fervor to overwhelm his love and concern for his brother. As a result, I don't know that I would feel real comfortable being who I really am with him because he can be real judgmental. I am not usually like that around others, but he is my older brother. I wouldn't want to offend him.

Having the truth is a real double-edged sword. There is a tendency to look down on others when you know you are right. Feelings of superiority produce a subconscious desire to control others through higher expectations of behavior. That is an incredible power to hold over someone. Through personal growth, I have become more secure in the face of criticism and judgment. I still struggle with it in certain areas, where I feel I might jeopardize the thin thread of a relationship I still have with my older brother. I feel more comfortable with him now than I did ten years ago.

**What happened with your divorces?**

[Rick] I had two affairs that became public knowledge. When the word got out about them, I sensed a shift in the church's attitude toward me. As my ex-wife shared her feelings with church members about the whole thing, the church began to side with her more and more.

[Kari] Several people were disillusioned when they learned of my divorce. My former husband had been very active, not only in our local church, but in the conference and union as well. People did not know how to relate to us, so they just broke off contact. I guess I understand. I'm not sure what I would do if my friends were to go through the same thing.

What complicated things for us was that when Rick and I began dating, I had been divorced for over a year, but Rick was still married.

[Rick] I had been separated for several months and

was in the process of getting a divorce. Because Kari and I attended the same church, things grew complicated fast. Rumors started flying that Kari had wrecked any chances for me and my soon-to-be ex-wife from ever getting back together. Everyone just started backing away.

To complicate things even further, my mother died just before our wedding. On her deathbed, she disowned Kari and me. That was very difficult to take.

**Is this the time you both stopped attending church?**

[Rick] Yes. In six months, I went through a lot of loss. I was depressed to the point that I sought counseling. I had to give up a law practice in the Northeast I had started and loved. My marriage broke up, and my kids disowned me. That's when my family backed away. Then my mom died. There was this big wave of trauma that came over me.

[Kari] Because of our choices, people distanced themselves from us. In a way, the church distanced itself from us.

**What are your views of salvation?**

[Kari] To have a relationship with God is to be a kind person. Trying to treat people well is so important. I think that the Lord is pleased when we think of others.

[Rick] I am completely dependent on God for salvation. There is nothing I can do. I found the educational system at odds with the biblical view of salvation. If you follow the rules, you have a shot at salvation. Individuals who have the most influence on you are the ones who are constantly monitoring your behavior. Now that I'm dealing with criticism and judgmental attitudes better, I have so much more peace with myself and God. I can be a human being. It's incredible. It's freedom.

**Do you think that you two will ever come back to church?**

[Rick] I could maintain this peace I have within the church, but I don't think the church environment would nurture it. I don't need to be hassled by the right wing. I don't need to listen to their petty arguments over insignificant details they call truth. I do not need that in my life. They major in the minors.

Another thing I need that I don't think I would find at church is practical help in everyday life. One of the last sermons I heard was from a man trying to prove from the Bible and the Spirit of Prophecy that if you eat meat, you won't go to heaven. Not once did he mention anything about how being a vegetarian might actually improve my relationship with God because my mind would be clearer.

[Kari] I sense the need to go back. I have gone on my own several times. I would prefer slipping in the back, listening to the sermon, and then leaving. I would like Rick to go with me sometime, but that's not where he is at, and I can respect that.

**Do you consider yourselves Seventh-day Adventists?**

[Kari] Yes.

[Rick] Yes, but I consider myself a Christian who happens to be a Seventh-day Adventist.

**Is church membership important to you?**

[Kari] I do want to belong. It makes me feel good to know that I am still a member. Being a member gives me a sense of belonging. It gives me comfort. Part of me thinks about questions like "When I die, who is going to bury me?"

I want to have a funeral in a church that believes as I do. Beliefs like the Sabbath, the second coming, and Jesus as our friend are all important to me. I believe all these things. I just stop where the legalism comes in. I want my personal growth with the Lord to become stronger. Deep down, I believe that if I went back to church to grow personally, someone would be looking at me and judging me. We both went through terrible divorces.

[Rick] That's why I am still angry.

[Kari] No one ever came and knocked on my door and asked, "Can we help you?" or "Can we pray with you?" We were left out in the cold. I had attended on a regular basis up to that time. Not one person came, and that hurts. I still believe. It hasn't gone by the wayside. I still believe in the seventh day. I still believe in the second coming. I still accept the philosophies the Adventist Church preaches. I think [the members] are missing the boat. People who have a one-on-one relationship with God would have been different. I really pity the people in the church because they've missed it.

[Rick] Are you still angry too?

[Kari] Part of me is still angry about that.

**Are you both still members?**

[Rick] Yes. The last time we heard, we still are. It's been several years since we've been there, and now that we live several hundred miles away, our contact with that church is limited.

**Do you donate your time or financial resources to charitable causes?**

[Rick] We both feel that it is very important to help others through our tithe and time. We donate money to several organizations.

[Kari] ADRA [Adventist Development and Relief Agency] is one of our favorites. The humanitarian efforts really make us proud to be associated with Adventism.

## THOUGHT QUESTIONS

1. How did Rick's and Kari's childhood environments affect whom they married and how those relationships ended in divorce?

2. Some members of their respective families rejected the couple because of divorce. Did the family members respond in the right way? Did church members do the right thing?

3. What can churches and families do for their members when they are going through a divorce? Why do some church members side with one person and alienate the other in a divorce situation? Is this acceptable? How can it be avoided?

4. What do you think about Rick's observation that Adventism would not nurture his Christianity? What could the church do about Kari's desire to return?

5. Are Rick and Kari justified in still being angry, after many years, over the way they were treated during the divorces?

6. What do you think of their claims of still being Seventh-day Adventists? Do you see anything wrong with their giving habits?

---------------------- Chapter 6 ----------------------

# Kyle

## Age: Twenty-something
## Occupation: College student/waiter
## When he left the church: 1992

**Are you still an Adventist?**

I am. I follow the beliefs very closely. My mother has been an Adventist since I can remember. My father just recently joined the church. That's pretty cool.

I was raised to be an Adventist, and I attended Seventh-day Adventist schools almost all the way through. I did attend public school for six months. It was a real switch being in such a huge place. There were tons of students. I really missed my friends from academy. So I went back.

I really enjoyed the social system at academy. It was a pretty good place to be. Even now, I really miss those friends. On the other hand, a lot of policies are very contradictory. Hair, jewelry—they miss the point. [The faculty] end up being judgmental and condescending to students in their policies. Is this why we are here?

**How would you compare your upbringing to the**

*65*

5—T.W.L.

**world you live in now?**

I lived such a sheltered life. Now I work on the night shift at Denny's. Wow, I have seen so many amazing things. I had a man threaten my life with a gun. I have had lots of people threaten to kill me. I have been asked out several times by both men and women. I have met a lot of homosexuals. I don't agree with what they are doing, but I consider them friends.

When I was growing up, finding friends among faculty and other students was easy. In the world, you really have to work at it to discover who your real friends are. Life is much more complicated.

I had never encountered those things before. I had created in my mind what I thought about homosexuals and others. Now that I've gotten to know some, I have become much more tolerant.

**When did you stop attending church?**

I was a college student at a public college, my second try at public school. An Adventist college was nearby, and I would attend their vespers program because I didn't want to get up to go to church Sabbath morning.

I started dating an Adventist girl, and we just stopped attending. She was very religious. We were really tight. When I had to move back home, our relationship slowly grew apart.

Back home, I didn't go back to church either. I just got out of the habit. But there is more to it than that.

I had a lot of friends from my academy who went to school in that area. I lost contact with them over a six-month period. I feel as though I was abandoned by my friends. That really played a role in it.

I have tried to reestablish contact with one friend several times. He was real busy. As with my other

friends, after a while, I just gave up trying.
**What would it take for you to start attending church again?**
I don't know. I really don't know. I like church. But I am at a transition point in my life. I don't really know where I am going or what I'm going to do with my life.

There are some things in my life I would have to change. I am currently dating three women. I don't feel this is right. I also have some hobbies like war strategy and war simulations in which we use guns that shoot paint balls. I don't think that is right either.

I have so little free time. I work two jobs—it seems like I have no time for God. I only have time for me. That's wrong. It seems like all these things can take over your life. I am so exhausted at the end of the week. I don't work on Sabbaths, so I end up sleeping until late on Saturday. The boss at one of the places I am working [not Denny's] has been pushing me to work on Sabbath. I'm going to quit work there in a couple of weeks.

**Do you see the church making much of a difference in this new world you are discovering?**
Not a whole lot.

**What would you have the church doing?**
I really don't know what I would have them doing. Probably improve the hands-on involvement in community events. Talking with and befriending homosexuals. They really aren't that bad, if we would only take the time to talk with them. They are really afraid that they will be condemned.

Another thing I see when I'm working at Denny's is all these homeless people. Some of these people have lost everything and end up on the streets. There is a lot more of this going on than I ever imagined. I wouldn't know how to go about changing it—some wouldn't appreciate help very well.

**Are you happy?**

I don't know how to answer that question. Parts are good, and other parts need to improve. I guess you might describe me as the "stalled Adventist." I am still working on my future. I do not know what I want to do with the rest of my life.

**What are your biggest fears?**

I am afraid of losing my friends, my family. I am afraid of getting married and of not getting married. I am afraid of losing my hair. I guess I want to be known for something. I want to be remembered for the kind of guy people liked to have around.

## THOUGHT QUESTIONS

1. Kyle says that he has friends who are gay. What is your advice to him? Is this a good idea? He says that he is more tolerant now. Is that good?

2. Is Kyle lazy for not getting up to go to church? How could he say that his girlfriend was "very religious," yet neither of them attended church?

3. What do you think happened between Kyle and his friends? How do you respond to his observation that he felt abandoned by his friends? Should he have given up trying to make contact with them?

4. What do you think of the things he says are keeping him from attending church? Are they valid to you? To him?

5. What about Kyle's suggestions for what the church should be doing? Do you agree? Why or why not?

6. Kyle describes himself as a "stalled Adventist." Do you feel that many young adults are going through the same thing? What can older church members do, if anything, to help young people who feel stalled?

# Chapter 7

## SUSAN

**Age: Thirty-something**
**Occupation: Full-time homemaker**
**When she left the church: 1991**
**Married to Brent (chapter 8)**

**Tell me about your growing up and the kind of Adventism you grew up with.**
It was very family oriented. Our family revolved around the church family. Our whole week revolved around preparation for the Sabbath. We enjoyed Friday night because it was the time when everything stopped so Mom and Dad had to be with us. Then Sabbath we always went to Sabbath School and church.

Friday night we'd all study the lesson together if Daddy was teaching that week. He would usually discuss the lesson with us, ask for our feedback. So we got introduced to a lot of adult theological things early. We were kind of a cerebral family.

Saturday afternoon was always a crash-out time, when we could either stay home and crash, or my parents would pluck up the energy to go somewhere so they would not have to feel guilty about sleeping the whole afternoon away. That seemed to be a big deal, that if you slept all afternoon, that was kind of a slouchy way to keep the Sabbath. Then we'd go back to church for vespers, and after vespers there was usually some school-related activity. Of course, that was the big social night.

**How old were you when this went on?**

Really, from the time I can remember up through college. You know, my family switched in my teens, but the same program kept going even when my dad remarried. There was a six-month period when I was thirteen that my dad was like the big ex-guy, the marked man! But he got past that. Then when he and my stepmother got married, they kind of cycled right back into that exact kind of life.

**So how did his church treat him when he was going through that divorce?**

They treated him fine because he was always a very likable person. There was no discipline. He'd always been very close to the pastors, and he was on the church board. But there was no accountability. I do remember one instance of intervention there. I got up to sing in church one time and couldn't finish my song for crying because I was the only one of my family in church that day. I'd gotten a ride with someone. That one time, some ladies of the church came up to me and told me that they were going to find out what was going on. They took me back home, and they wanted some answers. But my mother was there—she was a basket case. But that was the closest that any of these friends of ten years came to caring enough to try to investigate at all. Dad left for another state, and we went with him. In that transition, he was almost immediately made an elder again. He was even smoking at the time, and the pastor knew it, but liked him so much he said he didn't care. And he was still on the board. I think he said they wanted him to be head elder, but he just didn't want that much responsibility. But they did know that was going on, Dad told me later.

**You went to an Adventist college. What was your state of mind then about religious things?**

I never really questioned attending the meetings and all the things that were going on there. I had a sense of wanting to be a person with more integrity than I had seen displayed to me. At the same time, when you've got a lot of emotional pain, you're so wounded—it's really hard to have all of what you're desiring. What affected my ability to seek after the Lord at that time was the all-pervasive idea of this gaping hole in my heart that I was trying to fill. I really knew it was God that I needed, yet my experiencing of Him in that area in terms of being able to heal my emotional and spiritual needs was—there was a void there.

I attended anything that was going on Friday night and Sabbath School and church. I never really found a lot that was dynamic about spiritual life there. I pretty much tried to keep my head above water but felt defective in everybody else's eyes.

I was determined, ever since I was in third grade, that I wanted to be a Bible teacher. So that was what shaped my major in college, which, as I think about it, was my main spiritual experience at college. It wasn't the worship time; it was the study that I was involved in for my classes. That's where I felt any spiritual nourishment that I ever felt. Even though my perceptions were clouded in a lot of areas, that was the closest I got to feeling some of my hunger and thirst satiated.

I was getting to be a little more of an "angry young man"

as I progressed in my religious studies because I heard all of what I perceived as the political stuff that goes on in a theology department. I don't think I was really clear on the Lord's voice back in those days, but there were a few times when I felt distinct impressions leading me in a certain direction. As I got close to my senior year, I started investigating denominational work, and I felt as clearly as I've ever felt it, even now, God say, "If you go into denominational work, you'll never know Me."

And I immediately said, "Well, then I'm not going to do that. I'll be a secretary or something. But I desire to know You in my life; that's my highest goal, more than being a person of position." That was the decision I made coming into my senior year.

**After you got married, you were still part of an Adventist church. What was that like?**

I would say that it was a growing time; it was certainly very necessary. Just as I needed the whole process of individuating from my family of origin, I needed to begin individualizing my new family, in our political views, our religious views.

My husband, Brent, and I were challenged by some non-Adventist friends. We weren't very active in church. Brent was almost an atheist at that point, he has said since then. We were very distant from each other in that area. Anything that even smacked of being spiritual, like praying together—I know that's hard for a lot of people—but any kind of spiritual tenderness was absent from our home at that time. If I tried to initiate it, he wasn't about to be made to feel guilty, and so sometimes it would happen in a very cold way. Other times, it would happen that we could have a little discussion in a very petty kind of way.

Then that year on my birthday, some friends of my sister's who were from charismatic circles, actually Episcopalian charismatic, came over, and they started praying over me, just blessing me for my birthday party. That was how they were celebrating my birthday. As they prayed and read things out of the Word, I was just crying. I couldn't believe how this was ministering to me and how I was getting these feelings of worth from these people spending their evening blessing me in the name of the Lord.

And then when it came Brent's turn to pray a blessing, he was in tears, and he said, "Lord, her heart desires to serve You, and I've been standing in the road preventing it. I promise I'll never stop her from serving You again." I mean, he'd never prayed a sincere prayer with me, over me, before. I just sat there unbelieving. We came back home from that and began to get very involved in the local Adventist church here.

I'll never forget what I got from a book called *Hearing God*, by Peter Lord. It was like, wow, I really can be plugged in; I really can know.

I talked to the Adventist pastor there at the time, and he was telling me what he was thinking about something, and I said, "Well, have you talked with the Lord about it?"

And he said, "What do you mean?"

I said, "Have you asked God? Have you really sought His counsel?"

He said, "Well, I pray, if that's what you're asking."

I said, "Are you hearing from Him?"

He said, "Well, I don't know. How do you know if it's Him?"

This was the beginning of my realizing that everything the Lord was doing in me was getting very out of sync with my surroundings. I wanted to believe the Bible literally, that when the Lord gives me a promise, I can claim it over my life and expect the miracles to flow—physically, spiritually, emotionally, all of it. I got an inkling then that this is afforded the life of a believer. And if I came more into that place of not wanting to play church but wanting empowerment, to really become whole and to really be conformed to the image of Christ, it was putting me at great odds with the other Adventists who wanted to just continue doing the church thing that they had done all their lives and didn't want anyone rocking the boat. They didn't want anyone asking hard questions. I didn't perceive myself as asking hard questions. I thought I was asking basic ones. But it seemed to really frighten them.

I'd been doing a women's Bible study on Mondays. I felt as if I was supposed to start this. Lots of women had come for quite a while. It dwindled down after about six months to me and one other person. As I look back on those days, knowing what I know now about the power of anointed, Spirit-led prayer, I see that that prayer time was so dead. It's amazing that people can keep it up for six months. The kind of prayers that were prayed, they were just so dry, and not even hungry at all. Just out of form, they might pray for whoever was on the sick list for the week. I mean, they weren't coming to the cross to receive life. They were coming with their want list. And I was seeking for something a little deeper, but I didn't feel that echoed in anyone who came.

We had been going to that Adventist church for three years when we visited my sister again and saw those same people who had prayed over us. One of them looked at me and said,"Well, you know, the Lord is going to take such good care of you, He's not going to leave you in that dry old Adventist denomination."

And I looked at him, and I was so offended. I was just horror-struck at the thought that he would be so arrogant as to say that, because I was going to be an Adventist until I died. I was fiercely loyal to the denomination, to the doctrines, and more than all of that, to the idea that I was not an apostate. I was a person of integrity. I was never going to leave the Adventist Church.

Brent read a book by a former Adventist, his last name was Slattery—I don't remember his first name—and I think he had gone into either Presbyterianism or Methodism, I can't remember. But I remember Brent came across the book in a bookstore. No one told him about it, and he wasn't hyped up or anything. He read it, and he said to me, "This is why it's so dead. This is why it's not bringing us new life. Read this." I read, and I just cried, because we had believed so tenaciously things that were traditions of men. They weren't the very God-breathed instructions of God that we had been told; they were traditions of men.

**Can you give me a couple of examples?**

For instance, the whole idea of last-day events. We were led to believe that Adventism was unique in all the world. I read some things that convinced me that some doctrines [the Seventh-day Adventist Church] had come up with were prevalent in mainstream Christian church thinking in this era. We were just kind of going along with the cultural norm in these areas. They were things that I was aghast at. I went, *I thought God showed [Ellen White] that in a vision or something.* And then I found out that it was just all ditto, this whole idea of dispensationalism. I didn't realize it, but about the only difference between the Adventist version of dispensationalism and Methodist or Baptist or Assemblies of God, any of them, is just that the others tack on the rapture. But otherwise, the gloom and doom and this ragged little band of struggling Christians that God will, by a miracle of His, preserve, even though they are just in shambles, the whole idea of this horrible end-time deal—I had no idea that that was born in all those churches around that same ten-year period [in the nineteenth century].

And that really hit me. Then when [Slattery] showed a copy of a letter that said that [Ellen White] was asking her son Willie to bring her as many cans of oysters as he could fit in his suitcase—I mean, that doesn't sound like a lot, but when I read it—as much as every *t* had had to be crossed and every *i* dotted in church life because of her writings all my life—it was like a cold slap in the face. It was like the Pharisees, putting burdens on other men's backs that you can't even bear yourself. That was the scripture that came into my mind.

It was those types of things that boggled my mind. When I finished reading the book, Brent said, "So, you ready to leave the Adventist Church when we get back home?" ( We were away for the weekend.)

I looked at him, and I said, "You know what? With all my heart I'm feeling led to, but I've never been so scared in my life. Can I possibly be an Adventist and have integrity with the Lord? I'm so confused."

But we decided that we felt the Spirit leading us away from Adventism. We prayed a prayer together. We said, "Lord, we're ready for You to change our friends; we're ready for You to change our beliefs; we're ready for You to change us. Just take our lives, and You can do anything you want. But we want to be holy, acceptable, pleasing to You, and we just give our lives over to You right now. We have no idea what we can possibly believe but what we've been taught, but You do."

So we left, doing major back flips about the idea of going to a church on Sunday. Oh, that was fearful then. I almost had a panic attack at the thought of it, because I just knew that I was going to go straight to hell if I went to church on Sunday. I had been taught that Sunday is the mark of the beast.

**Did anyone from the Adventist Church contact you?**

I wrote a letter for Brent and me telling them that we resigned all the positions that we held, that we were very sorry if it inconvenienced anyone, that we were in no way angry with anyone, that it was nothing personal, but that the Holy Spirit was literally leading us out of Adventism, and we had to follow. We didn't know where that road was going to take us. We just knew it was Him, and we had to follow.

The Adventist pastor (who was very dependent) was very angry then. Before that, he had called me frequently to ask me questions. With the last three pastors I've had until now, I've had that same scenario. They didn't call Brent; they called me. Now I know that was just totally out of order. Anyway, I remember he was very angry when he called on the phone. He was almost shouting, telling us, how in the world could we do this to him, that it made him look terrible, that he knew what the letter said but he knew it was because of him. I told him that that was not true, that the difference we had, we ironed out with him. Months before, he had yelled at me at a prayer meeting.

**Were you feeling any hurt because of things that had happened?**

No, I really wasn't. That one time, I made a comment in prayer meeting. I said, "I don't know about anybody else, but for me"—and he cut me off and said, "What is that supposed to mean? Is that supposed to mean that you're unique, and the rest of us are just unspiritual thugs?"

He just blasted me. I was pregnant, and it was all I could do to keep from weeping. I thought about it for a week, and I prayed about it. I called him and asked him to meet me a little early for vespers. I told him I wanted to be reconciled with him, and I wanted to forgive him. At first, he started into me again, and then all of a sudden he started crying, and he said, "You know what; you could have told everyone in this whole church about this and made a big ruckus for me. But you've treated me with grace and mercy that I didn't deserve. I just can't believe it."

And I said, "It's OK; it's OK. I'll need some grace and mercy next time."

So that was our only falling out. In my heart, it was gone after that. I felt really good that I could extend grace and mercy to someone who was in the wrong. Anyway, I was not feeling at odds so much with him as a pastor as I was with the entire Adventist denomination mentality. It seemed like every Adventist church I'd ever been in had the same "We're all run like this; this is the way we do things." You get a few radicals in there, and they just try to ignore them and hope they'll go away. Because the goal is longevity. The goal isn't power; it's longevity, to live your whole life in this calm

Adventist endeavor. As opposed to being dynamic temples of the living God that He pours His power into regularly. And you never know what's up His sleeve when He pours His power into you—you never know what He's going to be doing. "Hey, wonder what God's up to this week." That's never been, to my knowledge, a question in an Adventist church because, well, how stupid, He's up to the same thing He was twenty years ago, a hundred fifty years ago. God never changes; He has the same desires and purposes for His people.

[These Adventists] live their religious life with no expectation of blessing other than just to get through life. There is no sense of the miraculous. Like I said, I can only speak for the Adventist churches that I've been a part of. But that was what we were feeling, so it was not at all a break with just a pastor, although I'm sure we'll never be able to convince some people of that, because after we left, things got very bad with that pastor, and many, many people left.

**Did anyone else in that church contact you besides the pastor?**

His wife. I told her we disagreed pretty sharply with Ellen White's teachings and how they had been allowed to form doctrine. And she said, "Well, you know, that's kind of an old issue. You don't have to believe in Ellen White to be an Adventist anymore."

I said, "If you don't believe in Ellen White, I'm still baffled where you come up with half of the things that are believed."

As a student, I had read *Questions on Doctrine*, and I'd read where it said that the scapegoat was Satan, and I'd read that, going, *Now, wait a minute; how does this line up? OK, Jesus was the sacrificial Lamb, Satan was the scapegoat.* And I thought, you know, *I just don't believe that. That doesn't sound right.* And then I remembered that was a point in Slattery's book. He said, "Have you ever heard the line that Satan is the scapegoat?" And I'm going, *Yes, I remember asking myself that question.* And he said, "Did you know that Jesus was at once the sacrificial lamb and the scapegoat? He was both." And I thought, *Of course, He was both.* Satan never bore anything for me.

But his wife was the only one who has ever called me. The Adventist friends we had, from that time on, have all acted very afraid of us. We had people who were friends, and then we were just dropped off the planet. We kind of feared that that's what it would be like, that kind of rejection. We went ahead and believed that the Lord would keep all His promises to us to provide for our needs—one of those being friends.

**Wasn't there someone else who contacted you later and said, "I should have done this before"?**

Yes, there was. This one guy at the church, he's an eye doctor, and so because Brent and I wear glasses, we had seen him several times on a professional basis. He and his wife are still pretty friendly—you know, we're customers. She called me after maybe a year had gone by. I don't know whether some sermon had been preached that got her feeling guilty and emotional or something. That's what it seems like in retrospect, some guilt message from somewhere had been delivered to her, and she was acting on it even though she felt nervous and out of place about it. She said something like, "I know I should have done this a long time ago, but I'm just calling to invite you back to church." It might even have been when they were trying to get all the old Adventists back; I don't remember. Anyway, she said, "We really miss you, I really miss you, and I'm just so busy in my life that I can't possibly fit in seeing you any other time than at church."

I thought, *Wow, that's so weird.* I thanked her for calling.

Actually, we had been gone like three years when a guy called who I've heard from some folk is quite a fanatic. And yet just knowing from other people who are friends with him that he's missionary stock doesn't make him seem like a fanatic to me. He's not afraid of confronting strangers about their unhealthful habits— he's a doctor. He called and asked if there was anything the church could do for me, to meet my needs. The reason I liked him was because he wasn't out of the same mold. He wasn't "Night of the Living Dead." He was an alive, vibrant Christian who seemed to be interested in helping other people.

As I look back, the only kind of evangelism I absorbed from Adventism was one of wanting to make new Adventists, instead of wanting to set captives free. That's kind of what burns in my heart, because God has set me free from so much pain that I could have never figured out how to set myself free from.

And He's still doing it, every day, being faithful to just bring me to new heights of freedom in Him. So when I see people who are hurting or if I feel a prompt from His Spirit, not just my own do-goody mentality going wild, but if I feel a prompting from His Spirit, I don't feel reluctant to sing His praises or give Him glory if I'm out somewhere. More times than not, He really opens up opportunities to share Christ with people. Maybe not present the full gospel and ask for a conversion, but just to say Jesus is wonderful and just give Him a personal witness to testify, hey, He's almighty God.

I love evangelism because you only have to do it when He tells you to do it. When He tells you to do it, the power is there to do it, and certainly the enthusiasm is there to do it. You also have the receiver there because He orchestrated it all.

**Has your view of salvation changed, or was it right all along and some other things have changed?**

It has changed dramatically, because I thought it was measured, even in small percentage, based on me. If only 1 percent of my salvation is based on me, I would still be up a creek without a paddle. Because I'm just human. That's just been a wonderful thing, knowing that salvation comes as a 100 percent total free gift. Paul says neither height nor depth nor any other creature, persecution, tribulation, nakedness, famine, peril, or sword can separate us from the love of God. That was always my favorite verse growing up. I used to keep going back to Romans a lot as a girl because I really needed an anchor; I needed something in my life I was sure of that transcended my environment. That text always ministered to me.

But yet it was like the rug was always being jerked from under me from all the guilt that was being fed to me through the sermons and the literature, etc. Now in my understanding of salvation, salvation is—the initiation is—always from God, and then the response from me is utter appreciation for the undeserved mercy and grace God poured out on me. So my salvation is really, really sure, and the initiator of it was the sovereign God. I just have the blessing of responding to it openly, to the degree of openness He had given me at that point through His Spirit having softened my heart in order to even hear Him when He called me. So salvation is a very big thing for me now. My cousins were Baptists growing up, and their big question was, "Are you *saved*?!" We used to make fun of that question. We thought it was simple-minded. But now I think it is essential to the nuts and bolts of the question. "Are you saved?" And there's only a Yes or a No. It can't be "I think" or "maybe" or "I hope." You either are or you aren't. So I've thought that if anybody ever asks me that question again, I can say *Yessir, you better believe it!*

I remember one time in the last couple of years when I was studying Reformed doctrine. My grandmother always says, "Presbyterians, oh no. They're the people who believe in predestination." But you know, that's where our confidence is. Like it says in the Old Testament, some trust in horses; some trust in chariots; we will trust in the Lord. I got released into putting my total trust in Him. And also learning that this guilt and shame, it's all from the enemy. Guilt and shame have never, ever, ever motivated the righteousness of God. Never. The motivation for the righteousness of God flows out of a pure heart that's open to the Lord to use it.

Even as I look at my children and administer whatever correction I need to administer, the one thing I know that will not make them lovely creatures is to make them feel guilt and shame. We mature because we feel loved and for no other reason. New life begins to flow in our spirit, and we begin to be made in Christ's image as we begin to feel the love of God poured out on us. So, definitely, salvation is mine.

I think about the words of the songs I liked growing up, like "Leaning on the Everlasting Arms": "What a fellowship, what a joy divine / Leaning on the everlasting arms. . . . I have blessed peace." But I didn't know in my heart what it meant to sing them as loud as my voice could carry. I mean, when I sing now, I don't care who's around or where I'm at; it comes out of this well springing up in my soul, and I sing like I'm singing to deaf people. Because I just have to give Him all my praise and all the glory that's due Him, all the honor that's due Him.

That's where He has us right now. I can hardly believe that even though I was so scared at all these different transitional points along the way, what He had for me was peace and joy and just living right smack in the middle of His anointing. I think it's in Philippians 4, Paul says, "I want to lay hold of the things which Christ laid hold of for me." I was thinking about that last night, and I thought, *Lord, You've laid hold of things for me, and I don't want anything in my life other than what You laid hold of and planned for me.* So I feel content, peaceful, happy, knowing that I've begun eternity, and I'm really living with Christ seated in the heavens.

**Do you consider yourself a Seventh-day Adventist in any way at all?**

No.

**What would have to change in the Adventist Church before it would conform to what you think it should be?**

I'd like to reword that. If I saw a mighty anointing of the Holy Spirit fall on the Adventist Church, I would whoop and holler and shout "Hallelujah." But I would not assume that He needed me to go backward. I would still assume that He wanted me to continue in the

SUSAN 87

direction that He has me pointed, and I would praise Him that He was moving sovereignly to set captives free in that denomination as well. If I've given my heart to Jesus as my Lord and given my whole life over to Him for whatever He wanted to do and truly by His grace rested in the Lord Jesus, I doubt very seriously, in fact, I'm positive—I would stake my salvation on it—that I'm not going to stand ashamed at the judgment seat and be told, "Depart from Me; I never knew you."

I won't be told that on the basis of the fact that I didn't go to a church on Saturday. I know I won't. Because my rest is in Jesus every day. And I know that that's what He wants for me. I believe God could lift the cloud of deception and lethargy that hangs over the Adventist Church, and if He sovereignly chose to do that, I would be thrilled. My heart isn't for exclusiveness like it was raised to be as an Adventist. My heart is for "the table is set!" You know, go out into the highways and byways of the country and tell anybody who wants to come, to come in; the table's ready to eat. I'm not expecting that that invitation isn't going to be given to Adventists at some point, because God is so merciful. I really hope and believe it will be.

## THOUGHT QUESTIONS

1. Susan's father was liked by his church but not held accountable for behavior most Adventists find unacceptable. Is this lack of accountability a show of Christian love? Could it have contributed to Susan's perceptions of the Adventist Church later on?

2. Susan says she did not receive much spiritual nourishment at an Adventist college. Should the colleges pursue voluntary-participation spiritual programs more vigorously? Or should college students be left alone to grow their own faith?

3. How can Adventist churches facilitate the answering of doctrinal and lifestyle questions, given that many of them foster a climate of opposition to questioning?

4. How should Adventist members react to individuals who judge the church's message and theology based on their perception of the members' spiritual condition? Should mistakes of judgment be confronted?

5. How hard should Seventh-day Adventists try to pursue members who are pulling away? Is friendship an acceptable pretext for staying in contact and trying to draw them back? How should church members approach individuals who don't have strong friendship connections?

# Chapter 8

# BRENT

**Age: Thirty-something**
**Occupation: Aircraft mechanic**
**When he left the church: 1991**
**Married to Susan (chapter 7)**

**Tell me about your growing-up years.**

My dad, as far as I know, was an Adventist when he married my mom. I don't know how strong an Adventist he was. I heard that he wasn't one for a while. Then when he got into the church, he went to the point of neglecting his family to do things in the church, which was part of the reason he and my mom divorced. But I don't really remember those years up to when I was three years old. Then when my dad and mother divorced, my dad took me and my two older brothers, and we moved away. As far as I can remember, we were active in a small church there for quite a while. He still is.

He married my stepmother when I was about four. She had had a son by a previous marriage. He was probably six months younger than me. We all moved in together and continued going to the Adventist church.

At age eight, I started first grade. The reason I started so late was because my parents had read one of Mrs. White's books that said you needed to hold your kids back until they were a little older. So they held me back. I went to Adventist day school through the eighth grade. I was the eighth-grade class president, if I remember right. Then from there I went to an Adventist boarding academy.

My dad and I did a lot of things together, like playing and camping out. We had a boat and used to go out on the lake a lot. But I never really felt close to him. I always felt like there was a lack of knowing he cared, a lack of being able to tell me that he loved me. I just didn't feel close.

Whenever there were problems, they were more or less slipped under the carpet until they went away. Or if they were talked about, they weren't talked about around the family. It was taken care of behind closed doors, so I never really saw problems resolved. I just knew that whatever happened wasn't going on anymore.

**Was he pretty strict with you guys?**

Yes, he was very strict as far as discipline goes. He believed in using the belt. My oldest brother quit high school when he was seventeen and joined the army (with my dad's permission). Then my next-oldest brother ran away when he was thirteen. Apparently there were some bigger problems than I realized at that age. He ended up going to live with my mom for four or five years. He didn't finish high school. I think he got his GED later on, but I don't know if my oldest brother did or not. That gives away what kind of communication goes on in our family—I don't even know those things about them.

In the middle of my junior year, the youth pastor at academy held a Week of Prayer and preached on the second coming. He put the fear of God in me, and I decided I didn't want to be left out. I think I had a true experience and came to know the Lord at that time.

I worked with a pastor in the next state during that summer of my junior year. I just kind of helped out on Wednesday-night prayer meetings and a little bit in the church on Saturday. It was called something like "Youth Ministry for the Summer." Back at school for my senior year, everybody thought I would be wild again and want to party. But I didn't. And I had been elected the student association president for my senior year.

That year, I met a girl I dated for about five years. I think a combination of that and just letting things go slack with my relationship with the Lord meant I really wasn't pursuing Him at all anymore. I gradually got back into drinking and staying out late, a lot of the things that I had done before.

**After that, were you still involved in church anyway?**

Yes, I was going mainly because of my girlfriend and my parents. I felt like I had to hold to what I had told them before, so it was pretty hypocritical. I felt a lot of guilt over it. I always felt that what I was doing wasn't right, that the Lord didn't want me there. But I didn't really have the power or the ability to bring myself out of it.

**What happened when you moved away from them and their influence?**

I started technical school in a city two hours away. I would drive home on weekends to see my girlfriend. So I didn't really have a chance to get out and do anything. After

I had graduated from there, I worked at the airport near home for two years. I broke up with my girlfriend and then started doing some house remodeling for the government with my brother. Then I moved away from home for good.

I don't know if I was wild, but I had gotten to the point where I just liked to relax and have a couple of beers and just take it easy. I guess I had gotten over the craziness I had in high school and was mellowing out. Away from my parents, I didn't feel like I had to show anybody anything. But I wasn't doing what the Lord wanted me to do. I was still just doing what I wanted to do.

I met Susan then. Her stepmother and her father moved away, and we started renting an apartment together. We went to an Adventist minister for counseling, and he kind of figured out everything that was going on and didn't really say it was wrong or right. I guess he just figured we might as well get married.

I never pursued any kind of relationship with the Lord. I didn't feel like it was necessary at the time. We moved to where Susan's parents were, and I found a job. She found a job too. It seemed to be an open door. After a year, I was hired by a major airline. After a couple of months, I started realizing that I didn't really have a lot to look forward to. I had found the best job I figured I could find, and, after thirty years of being there, I would have nothing. I think that's when the Lord started dealing with my heart again.

Susan's sister had had a conversion and was going to an Episcopal church that was fairly charismatic. We visited her on Susan's birthday, and some people were there from her church. All they did was give her a blessing for her birthday. It went around the room, and then it came to me, and I told her that I felt I was the one who had been hindering her from having a relationship with the Lord, and I didn't want to do that anymore.

From there, the Lord really started dealing with us, and we started going back to the Adventist church at that time.

**Tell me about those years when you were active in an Adventist church.**

Between the time we came back from her birthday until the time we really started going to church, I was still really fighting it but also wanting it. I was an agnostic and didn't really know if there was a God, and if there was, I didn't know if He wanted to have anything to do with me.

Eventually, I did come to believe in Him and felt like I needed to have a relationship with Him. I wasn't sure how He felt about me at the time, but I knew I needed to go to church. So we started going to the Adventist church. I became a deacon and was teaching a Sabbath School class.

We had been going there about a year when I started talking to some of the guys at work who were Christians and realized that these guys knew their Bible and had a real relationship with the Lord. It shocked me because I had never been exposed to any other churches, and I had the belief that—I'm not really sure where I got this from; it might have just been me; it might have been something somebody said at one time—I had the feeling that the Adventist Church was the only church that really read the Bible and understood it and really had a relationship with God. When I met with these guys and prayed with them, I realized that the Lord has more people than just in the Adventist Church. Some of the guys gave me some information to read that started leading me down a different doctrinal path than what I had been on before.

**So were you attracted to some things that you discovered? Did you see problems in the Adventist Church too?**

I'd seen the problems in the church, and I was starting to feel them in our church. I really felt a lot of legalism, but I soon realized when I got away from Adventist legalism that I was finding it about everywhere I went. It's not confined to the Seventh-day Adventist Church. But I think there's still a difference as to how far the legalism goes.

A guy at work gave me a book. It was about the seventy weeks of Daniel and the great tribulation. Basically, that book convinced me of a new view of end times that I didn't hold before. After I'd read that, I thought maybe I needed to look at some other doctrines. Along the way, I discovered some things about Mrs. White that I didn't like too much. I read some things she'd written that didn't line up with Scripture as I was reading it.

Through that, and through the prayers and the ministry of some people in other churches, Susan and I came to the conclusion that we needed to leave the Adventist Church. So we left and started attending a Presbyterian church. It was called the Authorized Reformed Presbyterian Church, or the A.R.P., which is fairly conservative and really holds to the Bible. I know when you hear Presbyterian, you think of some of the liberal churches out there, but this one really wasn't.

**How have things changed in your mind since you left?**

It's been a real growing process. I started reading a lot

of works of John Calvin, Martin Luther, Matthew Henry—I got his commentaries—and I started being exposed to some theology I'd never read before. So I got a lot of head knowledge then. There came a point when we weren't able to minister and we weren't getting ministered to at the first Presbyterian church we had joined. And there were some problems with relationships there. So we felt the Lord was telling us it was time to move to another church, and we started going to another Presbyterian church. The Lord began revealing His grace to me and also how much He loves me. His grace not only brings me to Him and saves me, but it's also for walking in Him from that point on. I learned that it's all grace, that if I don't depend on Him in everything, that I'm just not going to make it. Anytime I think there's something I have to give Him for Him to accept me, then I'm not walking in grace anymore. I like to worship God, I like to honor Him, I like to live a good life for Him, but I do those because of the grace that He's poured out on me. It's not trying to get Him to do something for me so that He'll love me more—He can't love me any more than He already does.

So I went from knowledge to grace, and now I'm really learning a lot about how the Holy Spirit loves me. I've always known that God the Father loves me, that Jesus loves me, but I'd never really understood that the Holy Spirit loves me just as much as They do. That's where I'm at right now.

**Did anyone contact you after you left the Adventist Church?**

The only Adventist we've really had contact with is our eye doctor. We only see him when we get our eyes checked.

Another couple we've been friends with a long time, we're real close with. He's a literature evangelist. Susan talks to the wife a lot, and when they're in town, we always get together—we consider them real good friends. I believe they know the Lord; I have no doubt in that. At first, I thought it would be kind of weird because we weren't Adventists, but they've really been accepting us, and it's been a blessing to us. Another Adventist couple in town, we don't do a lot with, but when we do, it's always friendly, and we have a good time. But none of the ministers or elders from the church really approached us.

**So you don't know what their reaction was?**

No, not really. We're probably still on the books somewhere because we still get mail from the Adventist Church. Our birthdays are still on the church calendar—we get that in the mail! They haven't really followed up on that, I think, like they should. I guess in a way, I was disappointed that nobody came, but in another way, I was glad because it would have been hard to explain.

**Do you think of yourself as an Adventist in any way? Is there anything left of it?**

I consider myself an Adventist in that I'm looking forward to the second coming of Christ. I don't regret any of the things I learned in the Adventist Church, and I don't really regret my upbringing, because I know that everything that happened to me up to this point makes me who I am.

On the other hand, I really don't consider myself an Adventist anymore. But I know that the things I was taught for over half of my life really settled it for me that the Bible is the Word of God. The basic beliefs of the Trinity, the virgin birth, that sort of thing, I still hold to.

So, in that sense, I do have some things in common with the Adventist Church.

It's kind of weird. When people mention Seventh-day Adventists, there's a part of me that says, "Yes, I'm one of those," and then there's another part of me that says, "No, I'm not anymore."

**When you grow up around the Adventist Church, it's hard to just wipe it out, isn't it?**

We didn't have a hard time changing our doctrinal beliefs, but the Sabbath belief was one we really struggled with. Especially because of how it plays in the end-times view that Adventists hold. It was kind of scary to us for a while until we read Hebrews 4, which basically says that Jesus is the Sabbath. At least, that's the way we came to believe. So, in that sense, since we're in Christ, we feel like we're keeping the Sabbath in Him.

**What would have to change in the Adventist Church for it to be acceptable to you?**

That's a tough one, because they could change a lot of their doctrinal views, they could even start going to church on Sunday—I don't know what would cause me to want to go back. The Lord would have to tell me that's where He wanted me to go.

It's like a lot of other churches around. There's a lot of churches that I wouldn't go to because it's not where I am with the Lord right now. I really feel like there's a lot of legalism in the Adventist Church. I think there's probably legalism in the denomination I'm in right now, but in the local church we attend right now, I don't feel that. When I was in the Adventist Church, you felt it in every church you went to, at least I did.

When we were in the A.R.P. Presbyterian Church, we visited one of those churches in another state, and it was just as dead as dead can be. I wouldn't have gone to that church if I'd lived in that town. So I felt the differences in churches in that denomination. I haven't been in any other churches in the denomination I'm in now, so I don't really know what the overall spirit of it is. I just know what it is in our church.

**What do you think the Lord's working on in you right now, whether or not it would lead you back to the Adventist Church?**

He's working on my doubts. He's working on letting me be content in Him. He's teaching me about grace. He's becoming personal to me, so I can feel His presence. He causes my heart to burn to worship and to seek Him.

He's changed my desires as far as what I watch on TV, what I want to listen to on the radio, even what I want to read. It's not an experience I've had before, wanting to do things like this, which is really neat. I always knew I needed to be doing things differently, but it was hard to work up the desire. It's impossible, I guess. He's really been changing my heart. The verse where He says, "I'll change your hearts of stone to hearts of flesh, and I'll write My laws on your hearts," is really coming alive to me.

## THOUGHT QUESTIONS

1. Brent spent several years of his youth under a cloud of guilt and hypocrisy. Could anyone in the church have helped him to overcome those problems?

2. Is his father's emotional distance responsible for him moving away from the church? What about his father's tendency to hide problems?

3. When Brent began to search for the Lord again, what do you think attracted him to the spiritual experience of his workmates?

4. How do you respond to charges that Ellen White's writings do not always harmonize with the Bible? How would you prove that they do? What approach would you take to convince an unbeliever?

5. Is it God's Spirit who has convinced Brent to change his lifestyle habits?

6. Can God accept a believer who is sincerely seeking Him but rejects the seventh-day Sabbath? What could you say to someone to help them accept the Sabbath without hurting their relationship to God?

Chapter 9

# Ellen

**Age: Twenty-something**
**Occupation: Health-care worker**
**When she left the church: 1989**

**What kind of upbringing did you have?**

Both of my parents were raised Adventists, so I grew up in a typical Adventist home. I started church school in fourth grade and went to Adventist schools up through high school. The only thing somewhat different about my upbringing was that my parents did not have a regimented attitude about Adventism. It wasn't a huge crisis if we didn't go to church *every* week. Sometimes it would be a family day, where we'd take off and go to the zoo or go on a picnic.

I also grew up with parents who didn't discourage me from having friends who weren't Adventists. My parents always had friends and people coming into our home who were not Adventist. Some of the kids I grew up with, all the people they'd ever really known were Adventist.

**So life was pretty routine during those years?**

I'd say so. My mother got very sick with heart disease when I was in high school. I suppose any big crisis in your life makes you question all your values and your ideals. But every teenager goes through that, whether it's because of some big family crisis or whatever it may be.

My parents raised me to not just take something on face value. They raised me as an Adventist and in the church, but at the same time it was like, "This is what we believe, but the day is coming when you need to believe this for yourself, not just because this is what we tell you to believe or your church tells you to believe or your teachers do."

**Your parents are both still active in the church?**

My father has been dead for six years, and my mother is still fairly active in the church. They were always regular churchgoers. Especially the last years of my father's life when he was no longer working, he would do more things like being Sabbath School teacher and things like that. When I was younger and growing up and they were both working, we went to church every week, but they weren't as involved with church, like being on committees, being a deacon or elder, or any of those kinds of things.

My mother still goes to church. I would say that she, being the wonderful mother that she is, even though I no longer consider myself an Adventist, still loves me and respects my attitude.

**What circumstances led to your moving away from the church? Was it gradual or sudden?**

I think it was a long series of things. I talked to my sister about this recently, and one of the first things that started to make me question was when I was in seventh grade and John Lennon was killed. We were discussing it among ourselves in a classroom, and my teacher made some comment about it. She thought it was good in a way because she thought he was a terrible person. She brought up that at the height of the Beatles' popularity, he had said they were bigger than Jesus Christ. I suppose that was one of the first things that really started making me question about being an Adventist. But it was a very gradual thing.

I suppose it's the difference between growing up in a home where my parents told me that it wasn't wrong to associate with people who weren't Adventist, and the parents of my friends who said that basically you didn't want to associate with people who weren't Adventist unless you were witnessing to them.

I have a number of good friends right now who are Catholic, and we kind of laughed about this because I said, "Well, you know Catholics are considered one of the great evils in the Adventist Church." I remember when I was junior-high and high-school age, I had a neighbor friend who was a Catholic girl, and I'd find myself pulling back from becoming a closer friend to her. Looking back at it now, I think I felt this guilt and pressure not to get too close because if I wasn't witnessing to her, then I shouldn't be a close friend to her.

Of course, I think any teenager goes through questioning all the lifestyle things of being Adventist because it's not just a religion; it's your culture; it's your life; it's everything.

Another thing was my father getting sick and being very ill. He was unable to work, and my parents had difficulties paying my school bill. There's all this pressure—"Here's your bill; you're not going to get your diploma, blah, blah."

In retrospect, I realize that's just the way it works. But at the time, and I suppose this is one of those big moments, I thought that I had heard all my life, "You need to go to school here; it's a Christian, Adventist environment." I felt that they weren't being very merciful.

My grandmother, who is an extremely conservative Adventist, thinks I left because of lifestyle issues. But it goes deeper than that. When it comes to how I feel now as an adult and looking at these things through a more rational perspective, I guess that why I'm not Adventist now has more to do with religion than just Adventism. I think religion puts God in too small of a box for me. The God that I grew up with my whole life in church and church school is just not the God I can believe in anymore. Adventism and other religions put God in a nice, tidy little box—that's the only way they can deal with God. That's human nature, but I think God is more than that.

I had a real struggle as far as whether I was going to believe in God anymore, have a spiritual life or anything else. I thought that if I had to believe in the God I was raised to believe in, I couldn't believe in God anymore.

To be perfectly honest, I think in a lot of respects the Adventist Church is very bigoted, very sexist, and I have a lot of trouble with that. I have a lot of trouble with the tenet of the church that you only gain salvation by faith. They're saying that out of one side of their mouth, and out of the other side they're saying if you don't do all these works, you are not going to be saved. That's complete hypocrisy.

**Was there a specific time that you were no longer an Adventist?**

I think it was just a gradual growing away. What I like to tell my mother is that if she feels any remorse about the fact that I'm not an Adventist anymore, it's because they raised me to be an independent thinker. That has finally come back to haunt them!

Over the years, I had been continuing to go to church, but it was a shallow experience. About two years ago, I started going to church again. I started because a friend of mine at work wanted to go to this one church that has a twenty-something group. They had a lot of social activities, so I started going for the social aspect. But I decided to keep an open mind and see if this group was going to fill the spiritual part of myself that I wanted to fill. I went for a while, about six months, but I found myself back where I started. I found myself seeing the same things in this group that caused me to remove myself from Adventism to begin with.

I guess one of my biggest concerns about Adventism is sitting in judgment of everyone and everything. In my own relationship with God, I don't have that right, and no one has the right to sit in judgment except God. I realize other churches do this, but most of my experience has been with the Adventist Church. When you cut through all the superficial things, what it comes down to is sitting in judgment.

Another thing they preach is "hate the sin but love the sinner." I think they could work a little harder on loving the sinner. I don't have anything specific in mind. A friend of mine, who left the church and has gone back, talked to me about how she resolved this for herself. She concentrates on God and doesn't concentrate on the other people in the church. I don't disagree with her about that. But I'm like, no, it's not just the other people you go to church with; it's also the basic tenets and doctrines of the church. I think they promote these attitudes of judgment and bigotry and sexism. In a sense, it's hate, and that doesn't accomplish anything.

The people in my life who made me feel like I wanted to have a spiritual life and a relationship with God were not people who preached at me or sat in judgment of me but people who were loving and caring, and it shined through in their lives.

**Has anyone come to you who's tried to get you to come back?**

Not recently. There was someone about six months ago, from the church where I still have my name on the membership rolls. I don't consider myself an Adventist at all; I just haven't gotten around to taking my name off the rolls. I suppose because I'm a little bit of a chicken and I don't want my family having a massive attack.

One person on the lay ministerial staff did call, and he talked to me in a very pleasant, nonthreatening way. But I haven't had anyone contact me since then. This is the church where I had gone through high school, and probably it's out of sight, out of mind. I haven't been there for so long. I'd seen people not know me when I was there going to the young-adult group. But I haven't had anyone else calling. That would be a long, roundabout "no."

**Do you consider yourself an Adventist in any way?**

I suppose what I consider myself these days is kind of an unorthodox Christian. I have a basic respect for Christians, but I have things that go against the general grain of Judeo-Christianity. If I were to write down what I believe spiritually and about God, there's certainly Adventist influences in there. That's how I was raised. Like, for example, life after death and Christ's second coming. But, no, I don't consider myself an Adventist anymore.

I remember my grandmother sitting me down for a long talk a couple of years ago, and she said, "Ellen, I know something that you don't seem to know now. But deep down in your heart, I know you're an Adventist." I said something like, "Well, Grandma, no. I'm sorry, but no."

**What's your view of salvation?**

As far as being saved and having a life in heaven, the only way we can get that is by accepting Christ as our Saviour, and that's the only way we'd ever get there. That's a constant thing you have to do in your life. You can't say, "OK, I accept God as my personal Saviour; now I'm going to go out and sin against humanity. I've accepted Christ, and it's OK." I don't believe that. You have to live a godly life along with that, doing your best to be good to your fellow human beings.

I don't think that not going to church every week and wearing jewelry or any of these things I was warned about—"If you do this, you're not going to heaven; you're not going to be saved"—are going to keep you from heaven.

**What would have to change in the church before you would go back?**

The church needs to change its policies about women. I have a real problem with the fact that only men can be called to the ministry. I think that's a lot of bunk. I think there's a general sexism that pervades the church. I have met some women and thought, *If there was ever a person who had the call to the ministry, it's her.* I think that is why the church isn't reaching people and touching people's hearts.

I think they're starting to work on some small things in the church that I had been attending. They're trying harder to say, "We want you to come here and be with us, not because we want you to be an Adventist but because we want you to share in God's love for you." That's something that the Adventist Church has been terribly slow to do. It's like, "Come and be with us; be an Adventist immediately." There's a lot of people hurting out there in the world. If you consider yourself a Christian, it's your privilege and your duty to try and share God's love with people. Trying to convert them to Christianity or Adventism or whatever denomination you want, that isn't the point. If you look at Christ's life on earth, the point is just showing these people some love. There's a lot of people in the world who don't have any love in their life. I think that the church needs to work harder on that.

Something that's come to the fore recently is the ballot measures in some states dealing with homosexuality. This is an area that I feel very strongly about. Regardless of whether you believe they're born that way or they shouldn't be that way or whatever, Christians in general, the Adventist Church included, are very slow to show any love or compassion. They're missing something there. I think this is one area where we should hate the sin, and I can say I feel that way. I don't believe that God created us to be that way. But I think we're forgetting that God loves everyone. We don't have the right to judge. That's God's job.

I know a lot of people who think you can't be a Christian and be a homosexual. You can't love God and be a homosexual. I guess they don't talk to the same people I do. The bottom line is, we need a church policy that says it's not OK to do those things, but it is OK to show love and acceptance. Not that, perhaps, the doctrine needs to change, but how they work as a church. I think you could say, "We don't accept whatever you may be doing, we believe it's a sin, but we still love you, and this is an issue that you need to take up with God. But we still love you, and we're still going to embrace you and have you be a part of our church family."

Those are the types of things that I would have to see for me to make any move toward saying, "OK, I can align myself with this," and call myself an Adventist again.

**Are there any changes that would have to happen in you before you'd be ready to go back to the Adventist Church?**

I remember somebody telling me, "Someday when you're married and you have children, your views are going to change." I'm not saying that might not happen, but as far as some of the things we've been talking about that keep me from going back to the church, I don't think that those things are going to change in me. I struggled for a long, long time to even get myself back to God. I was ready to just write God off. I struggled very hard to build the spiritual life I have now.

A couple of years ago, I was offered financial help to go to an Adventist college. I did a lot of long, hard praying, and I decided I couldn't go because being in that environment would damage the delicate balance I had gotten in my spiritual life again.

From my perspective right now, it would be a change in the negative direction to go back to the Adventist Church, instead of a positive direction. I want to keep growing in my life—how I relate to people and how I relate to spiritual things. If the church made some of these changes we were talking about, that might make me feel like I wanted to be back in church among that fellowship. Right now, I don't see any of that being fixed.

## THOUGHT QUESTIONS

1. Did Ellen's parents take an acceptable risk in pushing her to think for herself, or was this a mistake?

2. Ellen and her parents had non-Adventist Christian friends. Might the Adventist Church benefit if all members pursued relationships with sincere Christians of other faiths?

3. A lay minister called Ellen and tactfully invited her back to church, but she chose to say No anyway. Has the church done everything it can or should do for Ellen?

4. How do you react to Ellen's judgment of church members—that they are too judgmental and too bigoted? Should the church try to correct such perceptions among former members? How should it be done?

5. Should active church members take No for an answer from former members, or should they keep in contact with them and keep future options open?

# Chapter 10

# Your Church's Response

This chapter contains ideas you can implement yourself or bring to a study group in your church for discussion.

## 1. MIAs

With help from your church clerk, compile a list of the *M*issing/*I*n*A*ctive (MIA) members in your congregation. This list should be considered confidential. If you have a reclaiming ministry or prayer team, share the names with them—but emphasize the importance of protecting these MIAs.

## 2. Body Outline

Arrive at church one Sabbath about thirty minutes early with two or three rolls of masking tape and four or five volunteers. The volunteers (use children too) lie on the ground in various parts of the church (lobby, hallways, steps to the rostrum). One volunteer lays a tape outline around the bodies of the volunteers. The result will be an image similar to the chalk outline used by police at a murder scene.

Have the pastor, elder, or Sabbath School super- intendent explain to the congregation why the outlines of these bodies appear around the church. They will explain to members that our lack of response to those who have dropped out is the equivalent to letting our relationship with them die. Conduct a discussion on why people leave the church and what they can do as a church to remedy these relationship deaths.

### 3. Interviews

Identify members of your congregation who have left the church and have come back. During Sabbath- morning services, interview them about their experi- ence. Potential questions you could ask include:

• Why did you leave the church?
• Did you want to come back?
• Did anything prevent you from doing so?
• Why do you think it is hard for people to come back?
• What do you recommend to the church to make it easier for former or inactive members to come back?

Write your own additional questions to suit the cir- cumstances.

### 4. Reclaiming Ministry Teams

After you have exposed your congregational family to a couple of activities that raise their awareness of missing and inactive church members, offer a series of training programs that help equip people in a reclaiming ministry. Possible resources include, but are not limited to:

• *Reclaiming Ministry Newsletter* is a free quarterly update from individuals, small groups, and local churches across the North American Division that are involved in reaching out to former members. Anyone who wishes to get on the mailing list may simply write the Baby Boomer Ministry Resource Center (BBMRC) and request it.

• Missing Member Ministry, a three-part resource package. Leader's guide and a training video help make this program easy to use. To order, call 402-486-2519, or write BBMRC Distribution Center, 5040 Prescott St., Lincoln, NE 68506.

• Learning to Care, a two-part training program that prepares members for reestablishing relationships with former members. The church leadership retreat is a six-hour weekend event. It is coupled with a seventeen-hour Visitation Training Seminar that lasts two weekends. For the name of the nearest instructor, contact the BBMRC Distribution Center.

• Quarterly seminars called "Reclaiming Roundtable" are being provided via satellite by BBMRC. These are distributed over the Adventist Communication Network (ACN) on Sabbath afternoons, and each is a two-hour workshop designed to train local church leaders and reclaiming ministry teams. There are video reports from churches that have successful programs and plenty of time for anyone to ask questions and dialogue with the presenters via a special 800 number. To get the current schedule, contact BBMRC.

This year, BBMRC is putting out a new resource package that includes materials for advertising and organizing a special "homecoming Sabbath" when former members are welcomed back to church. There are six different models, most of them cued to major holidays like Christmas, Easter, etc., and designed to appeal to all unchurched people, not just former members. BBMRC is publishing this for the North American Division.

• Reclaiming Missing Members, a program available to pastors through continuing education. It is available through the NAD Ministerial Association at 301-680-6000.

• *Caring for Inactive Members: How to Make God's House a Home*, a book by Dr. Kenneth Haugk. Among the most practical, down-to-earth training available today, Haugk's program helps members discover biblical motivations for starting a caring ministry and the easy steps to take to implement it. Stephen Ministries can be reached by calling 314-645-5511.

**5. Bulletin Announcements**

Over several weeks, include the following information in your church bulletin in the announcement section, or design a special insert that draws attention to the dropout problem. Place a title like "Reclaiming Former Members" above the quote.

Week 1: More than 70 percent of those who "trust Christ" and drop out of the church are led to the Lord by a stranger.

Week 2: Almost 90 percent of those who drop out of the church were initially led to Christ by someone who perceived evangelism as a manipulative dialogue.

Week 3: Converts who remain as members of a local church are usually the ones who have developed significant contacts with church members before their conversion.

Week 4: Converts who continue in the church are the

ones who establish significant friendships within the church following their conversion.[1]

Week 5: One study shows that almost 50 percent of the people who have left the church describe their relationship with Christ as "good or growing."

Week 6: Many former members who leave the church are glad to leave. In fact, many of them describe their feelings as relieved!

Week 7: According to one study, only 10 percent of former Adventists express any expectations of coming back.

Week 8: Over 70 percent of those who have left the church say that not one member visited them after they dropped out.[2]

Week 9: Nearly 80 percent of those who leave the church cite conflict with people or groups. Less than one in five leaves because of doctrinal disagreement.

Week 10: It has been estimated that there may be between one to two million former Seventh-day Adventists in North America. Membership in North America is just over 800,000, and less than half of that number attend church at least once a month.

Week 11: Nearly half of the dropouts are between the ages of twenty and thirty-five. Another quarter are thirty-six to fifty years of age.

Week 12: Individuals in the missing or apostate group are three times more likely to be divorced and remarried and four times more likely to be divorced and single than the average active member.[3]

## 6. Prayer Meeting or Small Group Study

Use the book *Ten Who Left* as a group study. Purchase a book for each attendee, and study one of the stories each week over several weeks. Take advantage of the study questions designed to help the reader understand each former member's story. Come together each week, and discuss the questions as a group. Then decide together what you can do to reach out to former members.

### 7. Sabbath School Class

Dedicate one Sabbath for all your adult classes to study the dropout problem. You can use one chapter from this book as a guide, or you can have them study the dropout track below. Ask them whether they have ever headed down the track before. What can a church do to prevent others from going down the track? What about those who have gone down the track?

#### The Dropout Track

A. A cluster of stressful events
B. Subtle attempts to reach out for help
C. Pastor and members do not respond
D. Hurting member feels angry at lack of response
E. Involvement in church decreases
F. Pastor and members do not respond
G. Hurting member quits attending, expecting to be contacted
H. No one contacts them to ask why they dropped out
I. They try to forget the painful memories
J. They reinvest the time elsewhere that they used to spend at church.[4]

### 8. Things Not to Do

Here are the five most common mistakes made by members and congregations in their attempt to bring inactive members back to activity:

A. Sending a letter to former and/or inactive members. In fact, research shows that this method angers more people than it attracts. Phone calls receive a similar response. Visits, however, are the best form of contact because they are the most personal.

B. Stewardships visits. If inactive members receive a personal visit, a high percentage of these visits are so-called stewardship visits, in which the person or family is asked for money. This communicates to the person that their money is more important to the church than they are as a person.

C. The pastor makes the visit. Most inactive members expect a pastor to visit them. After all, it's perceived as part of their job. A visit from a member however, will mean much more. Sometimes the best member to make the visit is someone who knows the inactive member and their background. This is the stuff long-term friendships are made of. The reestablishment of old relationships is what member visits should strive for.

D. A simple invitation. Individuals sometimes visit inactive members in order to get them to attend church again. Most former members can sense this and may be driven farther away. The main goals of visitation should be showing care and reestablishing a relationship.

E. Visiting only once. Many caring individuals see ministry to inactive members as a one-time visit. But a series of visits is necessary to bring about healing and reconciliation. Some experts say it takes at least one visit for every year the former members have been inactive.

## 9. Visitation Tips

Kenneth Haugk, a specialist in the study of inactive members, recommends the following tips for those visiting with inactives:

A. Listen more than talk. You should spend at least 75 percent of your time listening. If you are talking more than 25 percent, you will create the impression you are there to straighten out the former member.

B. Listen with all your energy.

C. Care with your whole heart for the person.

D. Be patient.

E. Be genuine.

F. Throw out any present agenda you have. You are there to learn the individual's needs, not to prescribe solutions based on your presuppositions.[5]

## 10. Newspaper Ad

If you live in an area where a lot of former Adventists live (e.g., where hospitals, industries, schools, etc., are filled with former Adventists), take out a quarter- or a half-page ad in your local paper to advertise a special meeting. Invite former members to meet and discuss ways the church can improve its ministry. Choose a neutral location such as a meeting room in a well-known restaurant or a hotel/motel conference room.

At the meeting, assure attendees that you want their ideas and you plan to implement them as God leads you. And mean it!

## 11. Bulletin Board

Create a bulletin board that lists some of the misconceptions congregations have toward inactive members. Here's a list of twelve comments members might make if they don't know the motivations of individuals who have stopped attending:

1. They are lazy.

2. They have lost their faith.

3. They are apathetic.

4. They don't want to come back.

5. They want to be left alone.

6. They will come back on their own.

7. They will come back if you bully them.

8. They only need to be reminded of duty.

9. They will come back after a brief telephone call.

10. They need to be told what to do.

11. We don't deal with their feelings or try to understand them.

12. Whatever the problem, it's their responsibility, not ours.[6]

## 12. What's in a Name? Poster

Create a What's in a Name? poster. It will help members remember which names are appropriate and which ones may be misunderstood. Include the following:

**What's in a Name?**

Please remember that people who no longer attend church can be offended when referred to as:

• Backsliders

• Dropouts

• Apostates

• Fallen-away members

According to extensive research, the least offensive label is "inactive member." Even though we may have referred to our inactive members in other ways, help us create an environment that considers the feelings of each person with whom we may come in contact.

---

1. The four quotes above adapted from Joseph Alderich, *Gentle Persuasion* (Portland, Ore.: Multnomah Press, 1988), 98, 99.

2. The four quotes above are from "Upper Columbia Conference of Seventh-day Adventists—A Study of Apostasy." Berrien Springs, Mich.: Institute of

Church Ministry, Andrews University, 1981. Other studies have reached different conclusions.

3. Monte Sahlin, *The Dropout Problem in the Adventist Church in North America*. North American Division Church Ministries Report (Silver Spring, Md.: North American Division of Seventh-day Adventists, 1989).

4. Adapted from Kenneth Haugk, *Reopening the Back Door* (St. Louis: Tebunah Ministries, 1992), 113.

5. From Kenneth Haugk, *Questions and Answers About Church Inactivity* (St. Louis: Tebunah Ministries, 1989), 20.

6. Ibid.

---

## Conclusion

# WHERE DO WE GO FROM HERE?

To many Seventh-day Adventists, ministering to former members seems like trying to floss a wounded Bengal tiger's teeth—it isn't something you even want to try. Some even ask the question, "What's the point?"

The point is that the number of former Adventists in North America probably exceeds the number of active Adventists. That means millions of hurting people, adrift from the church we believe should be shepherding them into the Holy City. We have a special group to reach, the individuals who already know the great message of Adventism but have moved out of the fellowship of Seventh-day Adventists. Only with an attitude for action and with intentional planning will we be able to begin rebuilding relationships with former members.

Where to start? As with any problem, the best place to start is with God. We want to examine our relationship with Him and allow Him to show us what we have neglected. We want to adopt an open spirit that invites God to accomplish reconciliation through us in His way.

Given the high number of former members who have left because of problems with people, being better friends to our inactive friends and family may be the next natural step. We have to break our concern with gaining or reclaiming *numbers* and be concerned about restoring *relationships*. Each of us is aware of how easily misunderstandings come about, whether they are caused by offense or by neglect. When we commit ourselves to avoiding offense in the name of persuasion, we will become more careful with our words, looks, and attitudes toward others.

We also have to acknowledge the extent of the problem of inactivity and its causes. How does one go about creating awareness among members that will lead to healthier relationships in and out of the church? Awareness that leads to changed behavior is created one of two ways. The first is to communicate how large a catastrophe the church faces because so many members have left. The problem has been slowly building through the years, so most active members do not realize how small the North American church is compared to its potential.

If institutions suffer cutbacks and eventually die, some will see the effects of the catastrophe firsthand. This reality check, already at work in a few people, will move some in a direction of change. But a long-term, meaningful change will have to come from another, more intentional approach.

The single most important factor in overcoming the inactivity problem is individuals like you and me. As we begin to respond to this huge challenge, we will seek training, recruit help in our local church, and build a team effort to reach out to former Adventists within our circle of influence. We will influence the rebuilding of relationships in the church so that spats over the color of the drapes and over where Pathfinders should meet will not create rifts and alienate members.

There are ten ideas in chapter 10 of this book that you can use to create greater awareness among your friends, family, and congregation. Why not implement some of them in your church?

Start out slow by interviewing a former member who has come back to church. Interview them during Sabbath School or church time. Afterwards, you might use the bulletin announcements that increase your congregation's awareness of the inactivity problem. Next, use the body-outline activity to foster a desire to change your church's attitude to former members.

Plan a training session for those interested in starting a reclaiming ministry. You may or may not get a large group, but those who come will be committed to the cause. Or make use of the Reclaiming Roundtable satellite seminars. Without ownership of the problem among church members, you have a wounded tiger by the tail.

**Concluding thoughts**

Whether this book has left you angry, sad, confused, or moved, one fact remains—a majority of people who were once part of us are now gone. As a result, our church will never be the same. At best, we are incomplete without them. Why? Because they are still part of us.

Jesus prayed a prayer of unity while He was on the earth. He said, "My prayer is not for them [members] alone. I pray for all those who will believe in me through their message, that all of them may be one, Father, just as you are in me and I am in you" (John 17:20). We have good news for former Seventh-day Adventists. Now it's time to deliver.